On Anvils
of
Experience

Essays on Addiction, Recovery,

&

Everything in Between

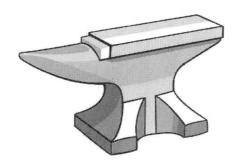

By David Lintvedt, M.Div

Dedicated to Those we lost, including:
Sal, Peaches, Satellite Mike, and Loaf

Also, to those who showed the way, Including:
Tom, Davey-Bop, Ted, and Al

And Too Many More to Count

Table of Contents

Introduction

Part One: What is Addiction?

Part Two: Collateral Damage

Introduction

So, what's this all about any way?

Substance Use Disorder (SUD): The *Diagnostic and Statistical Manual of Mental Disorders*, Fifth Edition (DSM-5), no longer uses the terms substance abuse and substance dependence, rather it refers to substance use disorders, which are defined as mild, moderate, or severe to indicate the level of severity, which is determined by the number of diagnostic criteria met by an individual. Substance use disorders occur when the recurrent use of alcohol and/or drugs causes clinically and functionally significant impairment, such as health problems, disability, and failure to meet major responsibilities at work, school, or home. According to the DSM-5, a diagnosis of substance use disorder is based on evidence of impaired control, social impairment, risky use, and pharmacological criteria. -- *Substance Abuse and Mental Health Services Administration (SAMSHA) Website.*

Substance Use Disorder (which includes Drug Addiction and Alcoholism) is a complicated disease, which can be difficult to understand. Doctors, Police, Judges, Ministers, Teachers, families, even the Addicted themselves struggle with the big questions of 'why'?

Why would anyone choose this life for themselves? Life as an Addict is filled with pain, torment, and despair, while there may be no bars or walls, this disease is a prison that separates us from all those we love and which is difficult to escape from without the help of others. And there is the even more heartbreaking question of why, after getting clean, does anyone willingly return to the life of active Addiction?

Why would a family, spouse, significant other or friend put up with an Addict's behavior, and still stick by them, still offer them support and give up a part of themselves to save someone who does not seem to want to be saved? Why go through all the stress and frustration, instead of simply putting the Addict out of their lives?

The truth is that these questions will often go unanswered and trying to find answers can be a waste of time and energy that could be better spent in dealing with the disease itself. Addiction affects everyone differently, but without treatment, the end result is the same: despair, frustration, broken lives, and a loss of hope, and this goes for both Addicts and the people in their lives.

As you read through these essays, there may be moments when you find yourself questioning why I feel like I am qualified to give advice on Substance Use Disorder…what makes me think that I'm so smart? The truth is that I am not all that qualified, all I have to offer is what I have learned on the "…anvils of experience" and the lessons were not always easy, as I have learned a lot from the mistakes I have made.

I have gained this experience from almost 30 years of Sobriety (as of this writing), as well as knowing what it is like to have a spouse (now an ex-spouse) and a child who have struggled with Addiction…and how helpless that can feel.

These experiences do not make me an expert on the subject of Addiction; however, it has given me plenty of real-world experience to share. I originally wrote these essays for the community outreach group I helped to organize: Project Live (projectliveup.org). These were published on the organization's Social Media pages, in an attempt to break the stigma, and to spread understanding of the impact Substance Use Disorder and the challenges of Recovery for all those involved.

I would be remiss if I did not point out that Addiction is not a 'one size fits all' disease, but can affect everyone differently, and we all have our own stories. When we share our stories, we will see that we are not alone, as most people have been touched by this disease in one way or another.

It is through sharing our stories that we begin break the stigma and shame of Addiction, that prevents people from getting help, and this allows us all to begin to heal.

As a person in long-term Recovery, and who has faced the challenges of having people I love and care for devastated by this disease, I feel that I have something to offer to those who are struggling. By sharing these essays, I hope to help those who are struggling, as they meet the challenges of Addiction face to face.

Many of these essays follow similar themes, and while I've tried to eliminate redundancy, in some cases I have let it go because I can, and I liked the piece. As I have been practicing the 12-steps since 1989, that influence is evident in these essays; however, I know that there is more than one way to get Sober. Another thing to note is that some of these essays have religious overtones…I hope this does not scare anyone off, as I am not here to proselytize, but I do hold a Master of Divinity degree, and have found that faith in a Higher Power (no matter how you define it) is an important part of Recovery.

And the bottom-line is that I am writing from own experience.

As with any other writing or speaking, upon review there are always things that I feel like I missed...that I wished I had said...but if I kept making revisions I would never be finished, so it is what it is.

I hope you get something positive from these essays, and please note that I will be donating 50% of the profits to Project Live Upper Perk, to help in their mission to break the stigma and shame of Addiction and to help those who are struggling.

Thank you for your support.

Part One:

What is Addiction?

An Attempt to Understand Something
That Can Be Hard to Explain.

1

<u>It Just Doesn't Make Sense</u>

Sometimes, it doesn't make any sense at all, especially when we see someone doing the same thing over and over again, even though it ends the same way, every time!

Years ago, I became acquainted with a guy who was the friend of a friend. I did not know him all that well, I can't even remember his name, but he as a nice enough person. He would occasionally go out drinking with my friends and I, or come to some of our parties. He was funny, and fearless (i.e. not very thoughtful, especially when drunk) which made him all the more fun to hang out with!

One afternoon, after drinking heavily with a different group of his other friends, he managed to drive home safely, despite being very intoxicated. Unfortunately, when he got out of his car, he didn't check to see if the street was clear, and he got caught up in the wheels of a passing tractor trailer! Somehow, he was not killed, but he was badly hurt, left in a wheelchair, with only a slim chance of being able to walk again one day!

When I saw him a few months after his accident, he could hardly move, and needed help with the wheelchair, but this did not stop him from drinking! We all took turns holding his beer while he drank it through a straw. Between drinks, he would puff on a joint that was being held up to his mouth! Even then, while I was still in the midst of active Addiction, I didn't think it made any sense, although some of the other guys treated him like a hero for continuing to party!

Over the next months, he had several surgeries and a lot of physical therapy, and a little more than a year after the accident, he was able to leave his wheelchair behind, and walk with a cane. A few months later, other than the scars, you would never know he'd been so badly hurt. During his recovery from the accident, he even gave up drinking and drugging, and life was looking up for him as he continued to heal.

As time went by, he felt better and better, and he got caught up in his life again, and although he seemed committed to staying Sober, one evening he found himself in the wrong place with the wrong people and was 'struck drunk'! Like many Addicts, he probably thought he could handle it again after being clean for so long.

And like many Addicts, he was wrong!

That one drink, turned into many drinks, and those turned into more drugs, and more trouble, and soon he was right where he would have been if he had never gotten Sober to begin with! Then, history repeated itself, as it often does. After drinking in the local bars, he became very drunk, but still managed to drive home without getting caught, or crashing. However, he didn't look when he stepped out of his car, and another truck came along, and took off the car door, which he was standing in front of, this time he was not so fortunate, and he died.

Even then, while I was still using myself, I wondered why he went back. I could see that Sobriety was working for him, and thought that if I had been through what he had, I would never touch the stuff again! But Addiction does not let go of it's victims easily, it is a disease that tells us that we do not have a disease, that the only people who have a problem with our drinking and drugging are OTHER people, we can handle it just fine!

Of course, we can't handle it, no matter what we think, or how much we want to believe our well-meaning friends and family members, when they tell us "...it's just one drink". This is why it is suggested that a Recovering Addict (no matter how long they are Sober) practice their Sobriety one day at a time, sometimes, ten minutes at a time...whatever works!

Some things just don't make sense...and Addiction is one of those, as it can lead those who suffer from it to keep doing the same things over and over again, while expecting different results...but never getting them.

Addiction does not let go of its victims easily. It cannot be cured, and no amount of will-power can save us from this disease, but there is hope nonetheless! Although we may often be at odds with each other, even to the point where it has almost become trendy, when it really comes down to it, when we really need each other, we can put aside our differences and help each other to face life on life's terms, and to not only survive, but thrive!

We cannot Recover alone, but the good news is: we do not have to, because we have each other, and we are all walking a path in life, and can help each other when the road gets rough!

<u>The Golden Hour</u>

It was a beautiful spring day, and we were sitting out in front of one of the campus townhouses.

The Sun was shining, it was not too hot or windy, the sound of The Grateful Dead was coming from the speakers that one of my friends had put in his windows, and we were sitting on sofa we had dragged outside, passing joints, drinking cheap beer, and taking hits off of a bottle of Jack Daniels!

Life was good!

I was with friends, having fun, and was pleasantly buzzed. This was my 'golden hour' when all felt right in the world, and I had just the right combination of substances in my system to feel content!

This was the moment that I chased for the rest of my active Addiction to drugs and alcohol!

I believe that every Addict has a 'golden hour', that moment when it all comes together in a perfect harmony: just the right combination of substances, along with the place and the people, that leaves the Addict feeling completely at peace and content! As the name implies, it does not last long, as sooner or later the high will either wear off, or the Addict will continue to push the envelope, to find a deeper intoxication, and the golden hour will be shattered!

I lost my 'golden hour' on that spring afternoon because I continued to drink and drug, lost that balance, and simply got very drunk! In time, I got the spins, and had to abandon my seat in the setting sunlight, to spend quality time in the bathroom!

While I still had some good times (yes, early on, drinking and drugging was fun – this is part of what hooks us into the Addiction) before the disease got the better of me, I was never able to have another 'golden hour'. I kept trying to get it back by using new and different combinations of drugs and alcohol, but nothing brought me back to that place! Instead, my Addiction got worse and took me farther away from what I was seeking. Eventually, my Addiction to drugs and alcohol that once brought me so much pleasure, and helped me to become a more social person, had the opposite effect. In the end, my search for the 'golden hour' left me withdrawn, paranoid, and miserable.

My story is not all that different from that of many other Addicts. While we often use our substance of choice as a social lubricant, and an escape from our troubles, we can also find ourselves chasing that 'golden hour', that perfect high that only slides farther and farther from our reach the more we drink and drug!

This search for the 'golden hour' is not only fruitless, but it is also frustrating and deadly.

However, there is hope for the Addict, because all that we were looking for in our substance of choice: freedom, acceptance, and happiness is found in Recovery! Becoming free of our Addiction does not bring us back to the way things were before we were addicted, but it does bring us to a new normal, a better, stronger place in our lives!

While life does not suddenly become perfect when we get sober, Recovery does bring us the opportunity for many moments of joy, love and contentment, far beyond those of any 'golden hour'. And for those times that are not so wonderful, Recovery gives us the tools to manage life, so that we no longer feel the need to escape, but have the courage to face the challenges of life.

Although Recovery is a gift that is available to anyone who seeks it, taking that first step can be difficult, and once Sober, the lure of finding that 'golden hour' again can be powerful enough to pull the Addict out of their Recovery, especially when times get tough...which they will. This is why the journey of Sobriety is more successful when it is shared with others who understand, those who have experienced Addiction and Sobriety for themselves, and who know every twist, turn, and hazard of the road.

It is when we help each other that we can find healing from Addiction, but first we need to speak the truth, to break the stigma that keeps this disease hidden away in the darkness, and to ask for help, and then take advantage of that help when it is offered, and to do so without shame.

When the denial and stigma of Addiction is broken, those who struggle can find the freedom to ask for and accept the help that is theirs for the taking...and it is in Recovery that we can truly find our 'golden hours'!

And these hours will not be fleeting!

Hard-Wired

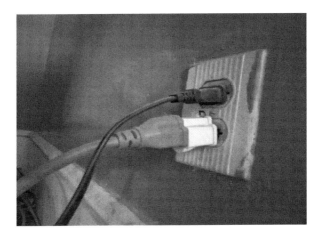

Someone who is addicted to drugs and/or alcohol is hard-wired to use their drug of choice – whether times are good or bad, when a change happens, often our first instinct is to use...it's our fallback!

These behaviors are deeply ingrained in us, for both the Addict and those who have been impacted by their disease.

This is why it is important to practice our Recovery on a daily basis.

An Addict is hard-wired to drink and/or drug

An Addict is hard-wired to drink or drug, whether times are good or bad, an Addict's instinct is to use their drug of choice!

This is why it is important for an Addict to practice their Recovery on a daily basis, because this is a disease that can go into remission, but never entirely go away!

And we need the support of other Sober people as well as the other people in our lives, if our Recovery is going to be successful!

Addiction is a hard disease to understand, even for those who have it!

It is a disease that tells the Addict that they don't have a problem, everyone else does! No one wants to be addicted to drugs or alcohol, but once it gets into the system of someone prone to the disease, it is often too late! It's like turning on a faucet and then breaking off the handle...there's no way to turn it off, not without help!

This is why someone addicted to drugs and/or alcohol can never go back to using 'normally'; we can't go back to just having one drink, one pill, or one toke...there is no such thing as moderation, only abstinence will work, and for that to work, we need the support of all those around us!

It Can't Happen to Me!

When we are young we can think we're invincible, like no matter what we do, we'll be fine! Because it can't happen to me!

Growing up today, kids are made aware of the dangers of abusing drugs and alcohol. There are TV shows, school programs like DARE, stories of overdose deaths are in the news, and people are more open about their experiences now as the stigma is breaking.

If anyone says that they were not warned about the dangers of drugs and alcohol, it simply doesn't ring true.

So, if the risk is clearly evident, why would anyone choose to pick up a drink or a drug, when they should know better? A big part of it is curiosity, kids have heard so much about the effects of drinking and drugging, that they want to see for themselves. They may also have friends or family members who use these substances, and seem to be doing just fine! And, of course, there is that belief "It can't happen to me!"

The first time someone uses, it may be a choice! Often the offer comes from someone who is trusted, who may even say "Just once won't hurt you!" (It should be noted that often, the people making the offer believe they are being nice, sharing something they enjoy with others!) The sad thing is, that if someone is prone to Addiction, it is the first drink or drug that dooms them to a life of struggle, as once an Addict takes that first drink or drug, there is no more choice!

In the clutches of Addiction, those afflicted are constantly seeking a better and bigger high, especially as their tolerance increases! This is why some Addicts will hear of an overdose and want to try that drug for themselves, thinking "This stuff must be really good, because it killed someone...but that won't happen to me!"

Unfortunately, an active Addiction can override common sense, and cause someone to overestimate their ability to handle their drug of choice, and this does not often end well!

While it is possible to understand how their disease can drive an Addict to disaster, it is when an Addict who has been in Recovery, starts using again, the we become truly puzzled! Why would anyone choose to go back to this life after some time Sober?

The majority of people who relapsed have told the same story: first they stopped practicing their Recovery program, then they began to question whether they had an Addiction at all, and finally, they decided to try it again, believing "It can't happen to me!" that they will be the one person who is able to drink or drug 'successfully' after being Sober for a time. Sadly, it can and does happen to them, because the disease of Addiction never goes away! Even after years of Sobriety, just one drink or drug can wake up the demons and send us spiraling downward once again!

Addiction is a heartless taskmaster, and can control us in so many ways, impacting both the Addict and the people in their lives! This is why Recovery from Addiction and Codependency is never something we can take for granted, but should be practiced on a daily basis, making getting involved with a program of Recovery a crucial part of our healing!

It can happen to us, even if it seems it out of our reach! We can all find our way to Sobriety and a new life! We can escape the clutches of Addiction, one day at a time, but we it will take some work, hope, and faith that there is a power greater than ourselves...from God (as we understand God), to those who have been able to stay Sober and who walk with us on our journey of healing and help to show us the way!

5

The Great Remover

The disease of Addiction is a great remover.

Addiction to drugs and alcohol removes people from our lives through illness, incarceration, estrangement and death. It is sad and frustrating to see someone slipping away from us, to know what they need to do to save themselves, but to be powerless to help them or to convince them to help themselves.

The sad truth is that once someone has been hooked by their drug of choice, they are already lost. Of course, being decent human beings, we will want to at least try to keep them safe and alive, but unfortunately there is not much we can do to save an Addict who does not want to be saved.

If the Addict is in our home, we may be advised to put them out of the house or to not give them any money. This advice makes sense, but to follow through is not as easy as it sounds, especially if the Addict is one of our children. We might be afraid that to put the Addict on the street means to condemn them to an institution or death, and there is some evidence to suggest that this is true. Also, putting them out of the house will not lessen our stress or worry, as it will only increase our uncertainty, and even cause us more than a little guilt.

As for money, sometimes it turns to be a way to keep the peace, even though common sense tells us this is not a good idea (noting that when we live with an Addict, we do not always make the best choices).

So, what do we do when the Addict in our lives is being destroyed by their disease?

Unfortunately, there are no easy answers. The sad truth is that sometimes we lose the Addict to their disease. Often the best we can do is to take care of ourselves, to ensure that we do not lose ourselves. This includes knowing when we are in trouble and having the courage to break the stigma to ask for help. Fortunately, we are not alone, there are many who are willing and ready to help – to remove our frustration and pain, or to at least make them livable! All we need to do is hold out our hand and ask for that help, it will be there.

For together, we can offer support and compassion that can never be removed: the understanding of someone who knows what it is like to live with an Addict/Alcoholic, and how to deal with the loss that many of us may face as that person is removed from our lives...and share the hope that no matter what happens, there is healing for us!

6

<u>Never Just One</u>

I have seldom had A drink!

As in ONE single drink...I never saw the point to it! I didn't like the taste of booze all that much, but if I drank enough my taste-buds stopped working, and the rest went down like water! Besides, I did not drink it for the taste anyway, but for the effect, which was to get good and drunk! I saw no other reason for drinking, and this worked for me because once I got started, it was just about impossible to stop! It was like turning on a faucet and having the handle break off so that there was no way to turn off the water!

Even when drinking made me sick, I was still compelled to push through it until I either ran out or passed-out. It was not a healthy choice, nor was it pretty to look at, but I considered it to be a badge of honor...here was one thing that I could do well.

Just having a single drink was a rarity for me. In fact, when I tried to think of a time when I only had a drink, other than the first few times I drank, and the last drink I had (half a can of Miller Lite while walking from 8th Street my office at the World Trade Center) I came up blank!

Of course, there were times when I had to be careful about how my consumption.

When at a work party, I would limit my drinks until the bosses left, or got wasted themselves, and then fill up on as much of the free booze that I could! If that was not an option, I would leave to go find the nearest (cheap) bar, or just head home, where I could drink and drug in peace (and did not have to share).

At family events, while I did not get falling down drunk, there were times that I over-did it and had to stop...if not then I would wind up making a fool out of myself, like when I ran into a heating duct in my brother's basement (30 years later, and I still have the scar)! Even if I finished out the evening drinking soda, once I got home, the craving drove me further into my Addiction!

This is why I do not drink at all today, because I know that just a single drink, even after all these years, would be too many...and lead to my doom! It may sound melodramatic, but it is not, this is serious stuff! Sobriety really is a matter of life or death for those of us who are in Recovery. Active Addiction may not kill us right away, but if unchecked, it will wear us down bit by bit, and it is nothing to play games with!

When I started going to my 12-step group, the 'Old Timers' warned that it was the "...first drink that gets you drunk". Many people have trouble understanding this concept. For both Addicts and the people in their lives, it doesn't necessarily make sense...after all, when has one drink ever made us drunk? Fortunately, this was easy for me to understand, because whenever I had made a feeble attempt to quit in the past, it was always having "...just one drink" that sent me back into my Addict to drugs and alcohol again!

It is because we know the first drink or drug will be devastating that it is generally accepted that an Addict cannot ever return to 'normal' drinking or drugging!

Note, that there is plenty about Addiction to drugs and/or alcohol that I do not understand, even though I am a victim of this disease myself, and have been Sober for years. Every day, I learn something new about this illness! For Recovery is an on-going process, which is constantly teaching us new lessons, because Addiction is not a disease that can be cured, but it can be managed and put into remission.

While this may seem daunting, as if there is no end to the struggle, this is not the case. Sobriety is not a long slow march through the mud, but sets us on a new path in our lives, one that frees us from the chains of Addiction, and therefore, offers us hope! In this light, it is best that we don't know everything about the disease of Addiction, this makes the idea of practicing Recovery much more meaningful, and leaves minds open to learning.

Practicing recovery from Addiction gives us great resources that can help us to meet any challenges that life puts in our way, without falling back to our habits.

One of the most important resources we gain from practicing Recovery, is the support and compassion we share with each other. Not only the people who have walked the same path and understand our struggles, but also those people who have always been there for us, our friends, family and partners. This also includes employers, and professionals, like counselors, teachers, clergy and doctors.

These are the people who will help us to stay away from that first drink or drug, which is the key to Recovery, for an Addict has to take that first drink or drug to get drunk or high. When we turn away from having A drink or A drug, one day at time, the rest of our life opens up with unlimited possibilities!

Priorities

I chose getting drunk and stoned over food!

The summer after I graduated college was a rough one, my temporary job fell through after two weeks, when the painter I worked for decided he didn't want to work for the summer! (or it could be that I did not do a great job, and he let me go...kindly.) This left me broke, and then the owners of the house where I was renting the attic, decided to sell, and I was told I had to get out within 30 days! (Note, that this worked out, because I would not have been able to pay the rent anyway.)

At my lowest point (that summer), I was down to $.10, a jar of peanut-butter and half a loaf of stale bread that a friend gave me. It was only a few days before I had to move, and I had nowhere to go. I was too ashamed to tell my parents or siblings how bad things were...and I was going to get out of this mess on my own!

With no other choice, I had to sell my car for funds, and after several weeks of having nothing but peanut-butter sandwiches (jelly was a luxury), I finally had money to buy food! While I could have gotten a nice steak, some veggies, or a just about anything else...the first thing I bought was beer, then pot, and once these priorities were covered, I got some mac & cheese!

For several weeks, I had little to eat, and lost so much weight that my clothes were hanging off of me, yet my first thoughts were not about feeding my body but feeding my Addiction!

Shortly after this some friends found out what kind of trouble I was in, and forced me to accept their help, without them I would have been homeless. While life did improve, this would not be the last time that I chose my Addiction over my need for food and shelter before I finally got Sober!

This is the power of active Addiction: it makes itself the most important thing in the life of an Addict, getting to the point where we feel like we cannot live without our drug of choice! Addiction becomes more important than our work, loved ones, a decent place to live, our health, and our dignity!

This may explain why being Addicted is often referred to as being 'hooked', and why it is so difficult to break the cycle of Addiction in our lives, and why we cannot face the impact of this disease alone! We need the help of others who know our pain and who want to help. However, just as with my story, if we are too ashamed to let anyone know there is a problem, things will only get worse!

This is why it breaking the stigma of Addiction should be a priority for us all! It is this stigma that keeps Addiction hidden in the darkness of shame. For that shame is not necessary, because Addiction is disease, and there is no shame in asking for help when facing your own illness, or that of someone in your life! It is helpful for us all to come together as a community, because addictive Addiction has an impact on the entire community. It is as a community that we can face down this monster and give those who suffer hope! It will not be an easy road to travel, but the journey is so much easier when we travel it together!

In Our Own Backyard

We are in the midst of a tragedy!

People are dying, in our midst, from big cities to small towns...right in our own backyards! They are our sons and daughters, brothers and sisters, husbands and wives, co-workers, friends, neighbors. This disease knows no boundaries of color, religion or economic status. It is an equal opportunity illness that destroys lives and families, and if unchecked will lead to loss of trust, loss of money, loss of freedom and eventually, loss of life!

This tragedy is playing out in slow motion, as people are dying one or two at a time, but the loss is just as devastating, and so sad because many of these victims are dying before their time. The disease that is killing all these people is Addiction to drugs and/or alcohol, and it is a disease that thrives on our shame and our silence!

Silence in the face of this illness is understandable, as few want to talk about this disease and its impact on their lives. It can be an embarrassing, and uncomfortable conversation. However, having these uncomfortable conversations must occur to make change happen!

The disease of Addiction thrives on silence and secrets, the more it stays hidden the worse it gets for the Addict, and the worse it gets for those whose lives are touched by that Addict. While it is true that we cannot do much to 'cure' the Addict in our lives, we should remember that we did not cause it, and we cannot control it…in short, we are powerless, and that can be very frustrating. What we can do, is take of ourselves, but this cannot happen if we stay silent and ashamed.

If someone in your life had a serious illness like Diabetes, Cancer, or Alzheimer's, would you be ashamed to discuss their disease, and its impact on your life? Hopefully not, their disease in not a reason for shame or embarrassment. In fact, there are support groups that have been organized to help families and friends struggling with the impact of serious, life threatening illness on their lives.

Addiction is also a life-threatening disease, an illness that wreaks havoc in the lives of its victims and in the lives of all those who are touched by the Addict. Like any other disease, this is not something that we need to keep to ourselves, to keep in the darkness, where it will only fester. Addiction is a wound that needs to be exposed to the light to be healed. We need to have these uncomfortable conversations in order to heal, and when we do, we will discover that our situation is not so unique, in truth it is unusual to find someone whose life has NOT been touched by Addiction to drugs and/or alcohol.

When we gather together to share our stories, we find ourselves becoming more comfortable with these difficult conversations, as we break the stigma of this horrible disease. When we help each other face the impact of another's Addiction in our lives, we give hope to all, as we learn that it is okay to be frustrated, to not know what to do, to feel as if we are at our wit's end!

However, when we share our stories, we learn that we are not alone, that others have traveled this same path and can give us hope.

The Unexpected Storm

It was supposed to be just a few flurries, maybe as much as an inch or two of accumulation overnight, and nothing to really worry about.

With the reassurance of the TV Meteorologists, people headed out for their regular Saturday evening activities: out to dinner, movies, shopping, concerts, sporting events, parties, etc. They believed they had little worry about, the snow would not be that bad, and it was going to start late at night!

When the flurries started earlier than expected, no one was concerned. It looked kind of pretty, and a few folks even had fun walking in it, kicking up puffs of snow with their feet, and making snowballs as it began to accumulate on the cars. Only a few sensed that this snow might be more serious than expected, and the first falling flakes saw them heading home, hoping to beat the snow to safety.

The light flurries soon changed to a heavy snow, and the roads went from just wet to treacherous within minutes, as drivers, caught off guard, found themselves sliding and swerving, and several wound up capsized along the side of the road, blocking the way for many other drivers...who spent much of that snowy evening trapped on the highway!

Some wound up having to find a place to stay, at a motel, with friends or with family! Those who made it home, found themselves having to shovel snow and salt icy sidewalks!

What was expected to be a light snow, wound up dumping several inches, and causing a lot of chaos!

Chaos, by its very nature, is capricious, and can derail all of our plans, no matter how well prepared we may be. This can happen in cases of a weather forecast, as well as with illness, which can be like a storm that catches us by surprise!

This includes the disease of Addiction! Remember, no one starts out wanting to be an Addict, no one wants to destroy their lives and the lives of those they love! For most of us, Addiction starts out simply, even innocently...with a single drink, a quick toke with friends, or an experiment with pills found in a medicine cabinet! Many Addictions were launched with the words "Just once won't hurt you"; and while this may be the truth for some, for those prone to Addiction, these words spell their doom!

The tragic thing is that no one really knows if they are prone to Addiction until they take that first drink or drug, and then it is often too late, just as the snow can pile-up quickly this disease can take hold of an Addict's life with brutal swiftness! And once it does, it is very difficult for them to break free of its grip!

This is why the disease of Addiction is referred to as "insidious", because it can sneak up on us and drill into our lives and the lives of those around us, causing ruin and pain, all while telling the Addicted that they do not have a problem with their drinking or drugging...everyone else does!

Addiction is a parasitic disease, slowly devouring its host, while keeping us complacent through the constant lies and false promises that this time, things will be different!

Knowing this, we can dismiss the idea that the Addicted are weak. The fact that they can survive their disease at all is a testament to their strength; however, no one person can face Addiction on their own, it takes a group effort! Just as when a storm hits, we are stronger when we work together, to help each other not only survive, but to dig-out, rebuild, restore and to recover!

When we put aside our differences, we can learn from our shared experiences, and offer each other support as we face an illness that is impossible to understand, and unmanageable by nature!

No one person alone is stronger than Addiction, but together, we can support each other as we take the journey of healing, one step at a time! For it's when we come together that we can ignite the spark of hope that can grow into the bright light that can guide us all (Addicts and the people in their lives) to a new way of life!

What of Faith?

It has been said that "fear and faith cannot live in the same house" meaning that if we are filled with faith, there will be no room for fear! It is a nice saying and is not entirely true...as they can be neighbors, with fear constantly disrupting faith by playing its music too loud, yelling or simply banging on the walls!

This is why, when facing any challenge, especially one like Addiction, it is helpful to keep practicing faith, over and over and over again! But, this may leave us wondering: What of Faith? What is it, and do we need to follow a specific Faith in order to find Recovery? Often, these questions of Faith make it difficult for people to trust in the 12-Step and other support groups, as they believe they have to follow a specific faith in order to participate. Fortunately, this is not the case, as most of these groups do not require adherence to a certain Faith, but only suggest that those who want to get help with the impact of Addiction believe in some power greater than themselves.

Speaking for myself, I believe that all people have faith. Many have religious faith, others have a sense of Spirituality, some place their faith in science, nature, or the universe, and it can even be argued that those who are Atheist have faith in their own system of belief. And many people are just not sure...

I believe that the Higher Power (whatever that is) speaks to us in ways we can understand, and is not 'one size fits all' because, like the farmer in the mountains of China and the Corporate VP in King of Prussia, we all come from different places in our lives!

That said, I also believe that one way this 'power greater than ourselves' speaks to us is through the people in our lives! When it comes to struggling with your own Addiction, or that of someone in your life, it helps when we speak the same language – for no matter where we are, or where we have come from, having Addiction in our lives is devastating, and something we cannot face alone! We need help to face this monster, and that is why it is important to put aside the stigma and shame and ask for support!

And our best source of help comes from those who have faced this challenge for themselves!

The assembly-line worker and the CEO can find common ground if they have been touched by Addiction, having both struggled with this disease, they will be able to understand and learn from each other's experience. This sense of connection, of understanding, can give us faith that we are not alone in our struggles, and this faith gives us hope!

Where there is hope and faith, the noise that fear is making can be turned down, and often even quieted completely, allowing us to face the impact of Addiction head-on, so that we can begin to heal together!

And it is in working together that we can find the faith and strength we need to face the challenges of Addiction.

You Were More Fun When You Were Drinking!

"You were more fun when you were drinking!"

Recently, while watching one of the late-night talk-shows, I saw the host turn to his guest, who was also his personal friend, and say to him "You were more fun when you were drinking!" He then asked his friend if he couldn't drink a beer or smoke a joint just once in a while, now that he'd been Sober for a few months. The man just shook his head, and said "No, you don't understand how this works."

I have had similar conversations, and although Sober for a long time, they did give me pause to think, but only for a moment...and the truth is I was not more fun when I was drinking! I was sloppy, obnoxious, crude, and made many bad choices. I also spent most of my weekends sitting alone in my apartment, either getting drunk and high, or recovering. And I know that if I were to start drinking or drugging again, it would be as if I never stopped in the first place, i.e. not pretty!

While Addiction can be arrested, it can never be cured. This why there is no going back to "normal" drinking or drugging for a person in Recovery. It is impossible for us to have just one drink or drug, because once the substance is in our system, the disease flares, and Addiction will once again pull us down into the depths of despair!

For many, early Sobriety can be a real adjustment due to all the changes inherent simply getting clean, such as avoiding the people, places and things that could throw us off-track.

This is why we are counseled to avoid major changes for the first year – as Sobriety itself is such a drastic change!

On the other hand, those in long-term Recovery can often find themselves plagued by complacency, as they become caught up with living life on life's terms, doing all those things everyone else does like working, paying bills, raising kids, etc., but doing them Sober! For these reasons, both groups can be vulnerable to the idea that they can now drink or drug "normally", especially when this suggestion is made by someone they trust!

Of course, no one wants to be an active Addict, and once Sober, few really want to dive back into that life, but the draw of our drug or drink of choice can sometimes be overwhelming, which is why Recovery is not practiced alone. While the support of the people in our lives, family and friends, is crucial, we do not need someone telling an Addict in Recovery, that they can now "handle it". Nor do they need to be questioned about the need for continued treatment, or why they still need to "go to meetings".

Another recovering person would never say these things.

If caught during a time of weakness, these questions could cause an Addict to doubt their commitment to Sobriety, or even if they really are Addicts at all.

Note that no one enters into Recovery by accident, if an Addict feels that things are bad enough to warrant seeking treatment, there should be little doubt that they could benefit from Sobriety; however, it is common to question if they really belong.

To be fair, in most cases, these people are not trying to cause us more pain, nor do they want to throw the Addict back into active Addiction, they simply don't understand how this disease works, because they do not have the illness themselves (which is a good thing for them).

This belief that Addiction can be cured is common among those who do not have the disease. The truth is that Addiction is not an easy thing to understand, even for those of us who have it. So, the people in our lives can be forgiven if they sometimes seem insensitive!

This misunderstanding of the nature of Addiction, is why it is important for all those who are touched by this illness to educate themselves about the disease. We can learn about Addiction not only through studying what has been written about it, but also by talking to each other. When those of us who are Addicts, or who have an addicted person in our lives share our experiences together, we can gain a greater understanding of the impact of active Addiction as well as the challenges of Recovery.

When we begin to talk to each other, we will realize that we are not alone, and the shame of Addiction will be broken! Breaking the stigma helps us to find new resources for support, as it allows us to work together to find healing, and a way to move forward in hope!

And the further along in Recovery we get, the more fun we find life to be!!

There's A Bus Waiting

We called him "Satellite Mike", but I never knew his real name. I heard that at one time he had a family, house and a good job, but all of that was taken away by alcohol and drugs. He had struggled with his addictions for many years and had been in and out of 12-step groups, rehabs and detoxes. By the time I met Mike, the abuse had left him with brain damage, what we in 'the rooms' refer to as a wet brain, which is almost like a perpetual state of drunkenness. This condition robbed him of his ability to think clearly and this left him unpredictable: it was a little scary but also made him very memorable.

I would occasionally give Mike rides to and from meetings…and although this meant that we had to ride with the windows open (as personal hygiene was not high on his list) I enjoyed talking with him, hearing stories of his drunken adventures, and the fantasies created by his sodden mind. Yet these talks also left me feeling very sad, as I could see flashes of the man he once was…before the Addiction carried him away.

Satellite Mike he had been trying to find long term sobriety for years, but every time he would get a few weeks or months of clean time together, he would feel better and decide that his problems were not that bad, and he would go on another bender. Once he told me that he regretted not taking advantage of those opportunities to find Sobriety early on, when he still had a chance; but when I knew him, he was so far gone it was hard to tell whether he was drunk or not.

We put up with Mike in the program, understanding that when he disrupted a meeting, or flipped over a table at the diner, it was because his brain was pumping out bad chemicals. As a reward for accepting Mike, we learned a lot from him as Mike was a true power of example…a warning of what was waiting for us, if we became complacent, or let our guard down...if we ever came to believe we could handle (or even deserve) our next drink or drug.

When he was going to meetings and sticking to his treatment plan, he lived in transitional housing provided by a non-profit group called Project Hospitality, whose goal it was to help people who were struggling with Addiction. When he was not sticking to his program Mike would just disappear; sometimes he'd be in a hospital, once he was locked up in jail for a short stretch, other times he was just off on a bender, perhaps sleeping in the Ferry Terminal or on the streets of Manhattan.

Eventually however, he would come back to the meetings, looking sheepish, asking for rides, food, cigarettes and forgiveness. He came back because he knew that there was nowhere else for him to go.

Satellite Mike was living in one of these transitional housing units when he went on his final drunk. I never learned how much of what happened was due to the amount of drugs and alcohol in his system, and how much as due to the damaged already done to his brain...and in the end it really did not matter.

One cool and damp spring night, after being kicked out of a bar, Mike began roaming the streets of Staten Island, yelling at cars, and accosting passersby. Finally, he got it into his head to play "bull fighter" with city buses, out on Victory Boulevard; he waved his coat like a cape, and was heard yelling "Toro, toro!" Several buses missed him, but as he leaped out of the way of one bus, he landed in the path of a second bus, that could not stop in time, and he was gone.

In the years since he died, I have often wondered if Mike meant to get hit by the bus that night, if that was the only way he saw to end the misery caused by his damaged brain, and the horror of not being able to drink without pain, while not being able to get Sober either.

Our lives can be filled with stress, and hard choices, and things don't always make sense. I worry about my daughter and how well (or poorly) I have done raising her as a single father, my relationship, my job situation, financial troubles and the future; and there are times when the physical and emotional pain has felt overwhelming, and I would like to escape life on life's terms for a little while; it is at times like these when the bottle (or rather several bottles) can tempt me to go off track.

When I feel this temptation, it is memories of people like Satellite Mike, Rocket Jack, Sal, and so many others (in and out of the Recovery community) that we have lost to Addiction to drugs and alcohol. I think of all the lives destroyed, the trust lost and the tears shed, and though I am sad for their loss, I am grateful for the lesson they taught me…that it doesn't get any better out there.

I also think of those who faced tragedy and unimaginable pain in their lives, like Al, Ted, Anne Marie and so many others who did not give in to their pain and were able to stay sober and help their loved ones heal. Through their example they taught us that while it can be difficult at times, life is good and better faced head on, and Sober; because Sober we do not have to face the challenges of life alone, because God is always with us, in spirit and in the example of those who have gone before us.

And that there is no problem that using will not make 1000 times worse!

It is these people who have gone on before us, who remind us that there is always a bus waiting for us to slip-up, and that we are never cured from our Addiction, but have to keep practicing it on a daily basis, so that we do not wind up jumping in front of our own bus!

That Sobriety is a gift we are to nurture and share with each other!

Part Two:

Collateral Damage

The Addict is Not the Only Victim...
Addition Impacts Everyone It Touches.

1

<u>The Three C's</u>

They are often referred to as the Three C's:

- We didn't CAUSE it – it is not our fault that the other person drinks and/or drugs, it is their private battle, and up to them to reach out to others for help.
- We can't CONTROL it – we have no power over the other person's desire to use their substance of choice.
- We can't CURE it – it is an illness that impacts its victims on physical, spiritual and mental levels, and cannot be cured through any known medical remedies.

When face to face with the devastation of Addiction, the Three C's can give us hope as they remind us that we are NOT responsible for anyone else's Addiction to drugs and/or alcohol, and that we have no control over this disease!

Logically we may be able to understand the Three C's and accept that none of it is our fault; however, on an emotional level it can it is not surprising that we can feel responsible!

Especially when the Addicted person is our child or partner.

We can find ourselves questioning our parenting skills, did we neglect to teach our kids about the dangers of drug and alcohol abuse, not pay enough attention to their friends, or were we just too lenient? We may also feel as if we were not there for the people we love and care for, asking if we gave them enough support or love? Wondering how we failed them, what we did wrong.

Trapped in this cycle of regret and blame, we can forget tha
necessarily facts, and that the guilt and shame we may feel a

This is why it helps to practice the Three C's, as they enabl
we are powerlessness in the face of the disease of Addictio
not a failing, but simply the way it is. This acceptance can ......
on the one person we can 'fix'...ourselves! While we cannot save an Addict
who does not want to be saved, we are responsible for our own healing,
whether the Addict is actively using or has become Sober.

Just as an Addict needs help with their disease, our struggle with Co-
Dependency is not a battle we can win our own. Healing happens in a
community, and when we ask for (and accept) help from those who have
walked our same path and know every twist and turn of it...and who also
know that while the road can be a rough one, it can also be the path to
happiness, and hope!

2

<u>Blinders</u>

Back when horses were the primary form of transportation and were crucial
to both farming and business, pulling a plow or a wagon, it was not
uncommon to see them wearing blinders.

Being on the dinner menu for things like wolves and mountain lions has
made it important for horses to be very aware of what is going on around
them, which is why they have eyes on either side of their heads. This gives
them an almost 360-degree line of sight, so they can watch for any dangers.
Being a prey animal also makes them very easy to startle, and it is for these
reasons that blinders are used: to prevent horses from panicking or getting
distracted by the activity going on around them!

...g blinders, a horse can only look straight ahead, and stay on task, ...ware of any dangers or reasons for fear. Blinders can protect a horse from ...anic that could cause the animal to get hurt, and also put the people working with the horse in danger!

As people with an Addiction in our lives, there are times when we too find ourselves wearing blinders, doing our best to ignore the turmoil that is going on around us, while we continue to do all we can to live our lives. This is not always a bad thing, just as with a horse, sometimes these blinders are there for our own protection, as life with an Addict can be overwhelming and frustrating. To be honest there is not much we can do for an Addict who doesn't want our help, who doesn't want to get better...and this is just heartbreaking, and not always something we want to see.

And then, there is the shame and embarrassment that comes with the disease of Addiction which can leave us reluctant to share our troubles with others, making it feel safer to leave the blinders on!

However, this is not good for us! When you have an Addict in your life, denial does not work, because Addiction does not just go away, the denial only makes its impact on our lives stronger. The best thing for us to do is to rip those blinders off, so we can start to see clearly, beyond our fear, pain and frustration, and begin to look at our own healing!

As always, the first step in this healing is to acknowledge that there is a problem to begin with. The next step can be learning about how the disease has impacted our lives, accepting that the only one we can 'fix' is our self. When we accept this, we can begin to put aside any embarrassment or shame and ask for the help we need! For in order to find healing for ourselves, it is important for us to come together with others who have struggled, and share our experience, strength and hope with each other, to know that there is hope and that we are not alone.

3

__Denial__

It's Not Just a River in Egypt

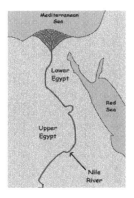

Denial is what we do when we are faced with something that is difficult to deal with or understand, and as a defense, we tell ourselves and those around us that it's not happening. While it is an understandable reaction, denial does not often have positive results. For example, if you were unable to pay your mortgage, and just ignored the late notices, rather than trying to work out something with the bank, thinking that foreclosure could not happen to you, it may result in becoming homeless. In that case, not only would you be hurting yourself, but also your family, and even the bank, who would pass on their loss to the customers who are paying their bills!

Denial in the face of Addiction can have a similar far reaching impact! Not only is the Addict hurt by this, as denial is a symptom of this disease, convincing the sufferer that they do not have a problem with using drugs/alcohol…it's everyone else who has a problem with it! This denial can lead to serious legal and health issues, including incarceration and death!

Denial can also have serious consequences for those of us with an Addict in our lives. Denial can make us blind to what's going on in front of us, but it does not take away the fear or frustration, this can lead us to fall into despair, which can leave us at a disadvantage when and if the Addict in our lives asks for our help in getting treatment for their illness. Weighed down by despair, we may not be able to offer them our support, as it is hard to help others, when we are in bad shape ourselves.

This is why denial can also be a type of survival strategy, albeit short-term. When there is an active Addict in your life, it is easy to become overwhelmed by feelings of powerlessness, tired of hearing the same old excuses and lies over and over again, tired of all the worrying and broken promises. In the midst of this turmoil, it may feel as if there is no escape, no fallback position where we can find peace! This is why, sometimes, being in denial can give us a break from the stress…after all, there is not much we can do to save an Addict anyway, so we might as well save ourselves. Unfortunately, denial is not a very therapeutic way of dealing with our problems.

Denial has a short shelf-life, because sooner or later the truth will always come out! When this happens, we can find ourselves feeling guilty for our inaction! However, it is important to remember that guilt and shame get us nowhere!

We have all fallen short of our best selves from time to time, but this does not need to be a reason for guilt, it is just part of being human! When we find ourselves dealing with the impact of another's Addiction, the frailty of our own humanity can become even more evident, leading us to make mistakes.

Denial can be a natural defense when faced with problems that are out of our control, but there are better, healthier ways to handle the impact of another's Addiction in our lives. We can start by admitting that there is a problem, by reaching out to others for the help we need to break our denial and face Addiction head-on!

This is not an easy thing to do, because facing life on life's terms can be scary, which is why we cannot face this disease alone, we need the help and support of those who know what it is like to struggle with Addiction in own their lives. People we can talk to about our fears and worries, because they understand, as they have taken the same journey.

4

"It's Only Booze"

"Thank God it is only booze, and NOT drugs!"

I have heard these words too often, when rather than looking at the problem in front of them, people will be happy that their child or loved one is only drinking and not doing 'real' drugs. Some parents will even encourage their children to drink at home, so they can keep a close eye on them, and to ensure they stay off of the road and out of harm's way after a night of drinking.

Of course, drinking is much more acceptable in our society than doing opioids. On TV and in movies, advertisements and in Social Media posts – *especially popular now are comments about the joys of drinking wine, which are aimed at moms.* Drinking is often portrayed as a reward, or something to be proud of, an accomplishment of sorts.

Recently, I was at an event where someone noticed I was not drinking and asked me "Why not?"

What a question! I have never asked anyone why they were drinking (unless I knew them to be Sober), but it is perfectly acceptable to ask why someone is not drinking...as if that were strange!

I am NOT a supporter of Prohibition, but it is true that alcohol kills more people than opioids (averaging 88,000 per year for alcohol, compared to an average of 30,000 for Opioids as of 2015). Although it is legal, we often forget that alcohol is a drug, and one that some people simply cannot tolerate! The unfortunate thing is that most people do not know that they are at risk of Alcoholism until they start drinking!

Just like any other addiction, Alcoholism is not caused by any failing on our part as parents, family or friends, nor is it the fault of the Addict. It is a disease that controlled by us, and it cannot be cured! However, the disease can be arrested, one day at a time, but the onus is on the Alcoholic to get help, as no Addict can ever be forced into Recovery.

Dealing with someone addicted to alcohol is just as frustrating as dealing with those addicted to any other drug. In some ones, it can even be more difficult because it is "just booze", but in truth, a drug is a drug, and alcohol is a drug! And, in many cases, alcohol is a 'gateway' drug, opening the door to the abuse of other drugs, as the Addict seeks a better and better 'high'.

Regardless of the substance, the pain we feel is just as great, as those of us with an Addict in our lives need help to face the challenges brought on by this disease. For we can be just as devastated by this illness as the Addict!

Although there is not much we can do for the addicted, we can take care of ourselves, and the best way to do this is to break the stigma of addiction to drugs and/or alcohol by reaching out to those who understand, because they have been where we are and we have been where they are now…together we can find comfort in the face of our pain!

And it is together that we can move forward!

5

<u>We Can't Know It All</u>

There are just some things I cannot make sense of:

I know very little about Nuclear Physics, if I tried to remodel my kitchen by myself, there's a good chance the Fire Company and the Ambulance Service would become involved at some point during the process. And for a long time, I thought the Theory of Relativity had something to do with how my Uncle Clarence would show up at our front door, unannounced, from time to time.

What I do know about is Addiction to drugs and alcohol. While I do not know everything about Addiction, I doubt that anyone could, I know that it doesn't make sense that anyone would believe that someone would choose to become an Addict, it is a horrible way of life, and once begun, our disease grabs a hold of us and does all it can to pull us under!

I have learned about the impact of Addiction on true anvils of experience! I have faced down this monster in my own life and found Sobriety, only to helplessly watch it tear apart the lives of people I love and care for.

Over the years I have had people ask me if I am really an Alcoholic, or if "...after all this time, don't you think you could drink normally?" I have also been offered drinks with "...oh you can have just one, right?" I have to admit, that there have been times when these questions have stirred my own question: "What if they're right?" However, I quickly put those thoughts out of my mind, as I know that's only my disease talking to me, as there is not 'cure' for Addiction...though it can be put into remission.

The people who have said these things are not bad people, who wanted to see me fail, they just don't get it. Which I tell them is a good thing, because that means they have never had to face this horror in their own lives, and hopefully never will!

There are many things I simply do not know, because I have not learned about, or experienced, these things for myself. This ignorance is okay, because no one has all the answers, which is why it is important to learn from each other, and it helps to remain teachable. If I wanted to learn about Physics, I would talk to a Physicist, if I needed my kitchen remodeled, I would hire a contractor, and there are times when it would be nice to see Clarence again, as he knew all there was to know about farming (and had a great sense of humor).

If I wanted to know about Addiction, it would be good to talk to professional who has studied the disease, to a recovering Addict, or the people in their life, who have all lived with the horror of this disease! These are the people who will understand, and who can offer suggestions for coping with the monster in our lives...and these gifts can give us hope, even when it seems out of reach.

The people who have walked in the darkness of this disease can be hand of help that puts hope within the grasp of those who have been impacted by Addiction! As we share this hope we are reminded that there is no shame in Addiction and telling those who struggle that they are not alone! Addiction touches everyone in a community in one way or another, from family members to first responders. Recovery tells us that this disease doesn't have to be a death sentence, as finding Sobriety can be the jumping off point for a new and better life...one that does make sense.

6

<u>Like Being Possessed</u>

It's like being possessed!

In movie The Exorcist, a sweet and innocent girl is taken over by a demon, who causes her to do horrible things to herself and others, as well as say terrible things to those who care about her! At first, her mother seeks help from both medical and psychiatric professionals, but nothing helps! Instead, the frustration and fear only deepen as the girl's behavior becomes more alarming and dangerous.

Finally, with nowhere else to turn, the girl's mother seeks help from the Church, now convinced that only an Exorcism will save her daughter. After some convincing, two priests are called upon to perform the ritual, yet this effort appears to fall short, as the demon will not leave the girl and instead mocks the priests. It is not until one of the priests tricks the demon into possessing him that it leaves the girl. Once possessed, the priest uses the last of his strength to jump through a window, killing himself in order to drive out the demon.

Like the demon in the movie, when Addiction takes hold of someone it will cause them to say and do horrible things and will do whatever it takes to justify their behavior and to feed their addiction! Just as with the girl in The Exorcist, those afflicted with this illness become possessed by it, turning them into strangers to others and also to themselves.

For those of us in the Addict's life, this change is heartbreaking as the person we know and love is suddenly taken away from us and we are left with a broken shell who lies, steals, breaks our trust, and doesn't seem to care about anyone...but they do seem very committed to their own demons.

This can leave us feeling afraid, frustrated and hopeless, especially if we have tired over and over again to 'cure' the Addict, even to the point losing ourselves, as this struggle consumes our lives, causing us to stop taking care of ourselves, damaging our work, finances, relationships and home-life!

Watching a loved one struggle with Addiction can be soul-crushing, testing our faith to the extreme.

Fortunately, in real life the situation does not have to be as dire as portrayed in the movie! We know that there is hope for an Addict, that the possession CAN be broken. Addiction doesn't have to be a death sentence, as the disease can be arrested and its hold on the Addict broken, although this Exorcism will not be easy!

The key to Recovery is for the afflicted to have a moment of clarity, where they will see the damage they are doing to themselves and all those around them, in hopes that this will lead them to want to get help; however, when and how the Addict comes to that moment is different for everyone...and some never get there!

Sadly, there is not much we can do to help them get to this place, no matter how much we love them, or how hard we try.

The truth is, when facing the demon of Addiction, we can only free ourselves!

The good news is that we too can have that moment of clarity, although it may be more difficult for us to admit that we also need help; after all it's the Addict to has the problem!

Yet, once we can break through our denial, and admit we need help, we will find that it is there for the taking! We can get help for our Co-dependency (not a bad word) from medical and psychiatric professionals, clergy, social services, as well as family and friends. We can also be helped by those who have trod the same stony road we have: other Co-Dependents, who truly understand because they have been where we are and made it through to the other side!

With their help, we can see that there is nothing to be ashamed of, as we did not choose to be possessed the Addiction, and that willpower alone cannot free us! However, this demon can be exorcised with the help of those who have faced their own demons and have not only survived, but also thrived!

For life is not meant to be a constant struggle, but lived happy, joyous and free!

At least that is our hope...

Just as we can be possessed by Addiction, we can be set free by hope!

7

<u>Saving Someone</u>

At the end of the movie Titanic, Jack and Rose are shown struggling to save each other from the inevitable disaster that is unfolding around them. The ship is sinking, and while its fate is sealed, these Jack and Rose are trying to save each other disregarding their own safety. Time and time again, as the ship was sinking they snatched each other from certain death, all while knowing that they will soon be in the icy waters enveloping the ship. Finally, we see Jack and Rose holding hands together on the stern as the ship slips into the ocean; they pull each other down into the cold water until Rose finally has to let go and allow herself to surface, in order to live.

Jack somehow survives and returns to Rose, with the ship heading to the bottom of the ocean, and survivors freezing to death all around them, Jack and Rose continue to try to keep each other alive. Jack finds a piece of the ship's ornate woodwork to use as a life raft; however, it is not big enough to carry both of them. Knowing that they will both die if they stay in the icy water, Jack lets Rose climb onto the raft while he holds onto the side until he finally succumbs to the cold.

 After some time, the shouts of the dying fade and Rose is left floating and shivering on the flotsam while Jack continues to hold onto her arm. When a lifeboat comes back to look for any survivors, with the sailors are calling into the darkness, Rose finally has to let go of Jack and let him sink into the depths, so that she can signal for her rescue. If she had continued to hold on, she would have died as well, but by letting go she was able call for help and be saved!

While the biggest boat I have ever been on was the Staten Island ferry, in a way, I have been in the same position as Rose was in the movie. One more than one occasion, I have fought valiantly to save another person, and my results were pretty much the same as Rose's were in the movie.

I have learned the hard way that I cannot save another person from Addiction to drugs and/or alcohol. All I can do is to offer my help, and to show them that there is a way out; but sadly, many people cannot see their way out of their troubles. What is even more heartbreaking, are those people who do not believe that Recovery is possible, or that they even deserve to be saved from their Addiction. It could be fear of taking the steps needed to be Sober, or maybe they simply some feel that they are beyond hope.

The good news is that no one is beyond hope or help. Help and hope surrounds us, and can be found in people who have been through the same trials and traumas that we are going through. Hope can be found not only in in professionals, but also in the caring people who want to help us make our lives better. There is hope in finding faith in a power greater than ourselves, whether that be God, the universe, a support group, or just those who care and can offer solutions and comfort.

There is always hope and help available, even if that help is not always easy to see or to take advantage of; if we feel that saving our own lives is worth the effort and yes…the possible frustration, then the struggle is worthwhile, and not as hard as it appears. My life was worth saving, but I had to want to save it, I had to want to work at making my life better and to get off the road to perdition and start building a new life.

Herein lies the rub: despite my years of sobriety and practicing principles, I cannot use what I have learned to fix another person, no matter how hard I try or how much I love and care for that person. When I have tried to fix a loved one in the past, my efforts have only served to annoy the person and to push us apart. Like Rose, it was only when I let go that I found peace myself. Some I tried to help never found that Sobriety, for others, it took several more years, and they had to pay a heavy price before they finally chose to get help and found successful Sobriety.

It can be frustrating to be living in the solution and not be able to help someone you care for find it for themselves. I have learned that sometimes all I can do is to live as a power of example, to share what I my experience with others (not force it on them) showing them that there is a better way to live. I can offer those who are in need of healing, my love, support and care. I can assist them in finding help if they want it and be there for them as they take their first struggling steps towards Recovery, but I cannot save another person no matter how hard I try or how much I love them...not unless they want to help themselves!

I have found that if I spend all of my energy trying to fix someone who doesn't want to fixed, I am in danger of getting lost myself, of being pulled down into the depths with them instead of bringing them up into the lifeboat with me. This has been a difficult lesson to learn, and one that I have to practice on a regular basis.

It is a sad truth that often we have to let go of those we love in order to allow them to rise or fall on their own. In the end, we can only save ourselves, and that is a big task all by itself. The good news is that if we choose to help ourselves, we do not have to do it alone, there is plenty of help available if we just ask for it! There are many people who have been where we are, taken the same journey, and are able to lead us all safely to shore!

8

Can YOU Fix It?

When I was in college, I worked for an airline that no longer exists.

Airline employees were allowed to fly for free if there were unsold seats available, being young, we took full advantage of this perk! Usually, we would show up early in the morning (on our day off) and see which Florida bound flights were open for us. One morning, some friends and I were on a plane heading to Tampa/St. Petersburg, when the flight crew announced we were being delayed due to a "Gate Hold"!

We knew that this term was sometimes used when there was a mechanical issue with the plane, to prevent the passengers from getting anxious. Being curious, I looked out of the window and saw a few mechanics working on the right-side engine of the 737. The cowling was off, and a thick stream of oil was pouring onto the tarmac, as the mechanics shook their heads. This did not engender confidence! Just then, one of my friends said "Why don't you go out and help them?" I declined, saying that I enjoyed being alive, so I would trust the experts.

Fortunately, the plane was repaired, and we made it safely to Florida (even though the engine buzzed the whole way).

My friend was only kidding, but could you imagine, being shown a jet engine on a commercial airliner, and being asked to "fix it"? I have trouble changing the oil on my car, trying to fix a jet would be a real disaster; however, I would do such a bad job that the plane would never get off of the ground!

There is no shame in admitting that I cannot fix an airplane, I'm not a jet mechanic! So then, why should there be any shame in admitting that I cannot fix an Addict?

As parents, we want to do what is best for our children, and if they become addicted to drugs and/or alcohol, it is only natural that we will want to fix them! We do not want them to suffer, or even die...especially so needlessly! That is why we can wind up beating ourselves up when faced with the fact that we cannot cure or control the Addiction of those we love. We can needlessly blame ourselves for letting things get so far off-track, and for not being able to stop the Addiction, to save our children!

While these feeling are understandable, knowing that they are 'normal' does not help us to feel better, or any less frustrated!

Unfortunately, just as it would have been impossible for me to fix the jet engine, we don't really know how to fix our addicted children, though we will try...we have to try! Even the 'experts' struggle with how to address the disease of Addiction, as Recovery relies upon the desire of the Addict to get Sober. We just have to trust the process and take care of ourselves, so that whether the Addict gets Sober or not, we will be able to survive!

This is so much easier said than done. That flight tested my trust as I kept checking that buzzing engine all the way from Newark to Tampa and was so glad when we touched down safely! In the same way it is not easy to learn to trust an Addict (even if Sober) or ourselves!

It does help to have faith in a power greater than ourselves, whoever we believe that power to be.

It also helps us to talk about our fears and frustrations with others, especially with those who understand the challenges we are facing, because they have faced them as well. These people can help us to accept that it is okay to be powerless, and that letting go of our children does not mean giving up or that we do not love them, but that we are choosing to fix the only person we can: ourselves...even if that means getting off of the plane and finding a new way forward together!

9

Enough Already!

To be brutally honest, sometimes we just want it to be over! When my father was dying from Parkinson's, it was like slow torture. Watching this man, who was a Math and Computer Science professor, intelligent, compassionate and funny, gradually lose himself in dementia was a horrible thing! And I have to admit, that there were some times when I just wanted the suffering to end: his, my family's, and my own!

I felt guilty about wanting it to be over, and I talked to a counselor about it. He told me that there was nothing to feel bad about, as it's normal to want someone I love to be out of pain, and to be released from that pain myself.

Like Parkinson's or any other degenerative disease, Addiction can also wreak havoc on our lives! If you have an Addict in your life, especially if it is your child or a spouse, you too may find yourself wanting it to all be over. You may be tired of jumping every time the phone rings, of being afraid when you turn onto your block, wondering if there will be police cars or an ambulance in front of the house. Tired of greeting each day uncertain of what you will find, will your loved one be passed out on the bathroom floor, missing, sleeping peacefully in bed, or no longer breathing!

Living in a constant state of stress, with no relief in sight can leave us feeling hopeless and trapped. It is natural to want to escape; unfortunately, this stress can lead many into substance abuse themselves, overeating or losing focus due to lack of sleep. This stress can cause damage to other relationships, cause trouble at work, or health problems...it can also cause our thinking to become skewed.

Although perfectly understandable, when we find ourselves wishing it was over, it can leave us feeling like horrible human beings, we need to remember that we are human, and can only take so much stress in our lives (in fact, it has been proposed that living with an active Addict can cause PTSD), and we cannot not always control our thoughts, especially if we are exhausted. Of course, we don't want any more pain in our lives, or in the lives of those we care about. Beating ourselves up for wanting some relief, or for thoughts we cannot control, will only add to our stress...and we have enough of that!

Fortunately, there are better ways of dealing with this stress. When our thoughts start to go to these awful places, we can practice turning our thinking around, by focusing on something else: go out for a walk, wash dishes, take a drive, visit a friend, turn to God (as we understand God), or simply pick up the phone and talk to someone. The key is getting out of your own head when it becomes an unpleasant place to be! However, it is not easy to do this on our own, this is why it is important to reach out to those who understand what we are going through, especially those who have traveled the same rocky roads we have trod.

One of the first steps is to break the stigma of Addiction, and we can do this by remembering that there is nothing to be ashamed of, Addiction is an illness and not a moral failing. Once we accept this it will be easier to ask for help, and when we do, we will find that we are not alone! The truth is that this disease affects so many lives that it can be difficult to find someone who has NOT been touched by it!

When we connect with people who understand what we are going through, we begin to let go of the stress and frustration and start healing. Just knowing we are not alone can make all the difference, as sharing our stories allows us to learn new ways to meet the challenges of having an Addict in our lives and find new avenues for hope.

10

<u>Frustration!</u>

Having an Addict/Alcoholic in our lives is very frustrating! We struggle to understand why they use drugs and alcohol, why they cannot see the damage they are doing to themselves and to us. We also look for ways to 'fix' them, or at least to keep them safe.

Wanting to fix someone we care about is understandable, it seems like the right thing to do.

Unfortunately, there are no easy answers. Addiction has been classified as a disease, but many still have their doubts; however, in the midst of the struggle the question of whether it is a disease or a weakness seems like a moot point! Our main concern is that the Addict in our life finds Recovery…but no matter what we do, nothing seems to help!

This frustration is not good for anyone, not for us or for the Addict, as it causes added stress we do not need, can kill hope and stall opportunities for healing.

The sad truth is that we are not able to 'fix' another person's Addiction/Alcoholism, no matter how hard we try or how much compassion and love we show them. The good news is that when we don't know what else to do, we can take care of ourselves!

We can start by taking the focus off of the Addict and onto ourselves, by looking at what we need to do in order to get healthy again. It has been noted that those who suffer from Co-dependency are often as ill as the Addict, having been overcome by stress rather than drugs (though some do fall into substance abuse as a way of trying to cope). This is why it is important for us to manage our own Recovery. This begins with reaching out to those who have been where we are, but in order to do this we will need to put aside the stigma and shame that comes with Addiction and Co-dependency, so we can speak up and ask for help in dealing with the impact of having an Addict in our lives.

Once we can speak up and ask for help, we may be surprised at how quickly that help will be offered. Many have been affected by the Addiction of others and are willing to share what they have learned to help others! With this help, we will get the support we need to start practicing how to let go of our fear and frustration, so that we can begin to heal, and in doing so, experience the joy of living for ourselves!

11

<u>Letting Go</u>

The Recovery world is filled with platitudes:

"One Day at A Time", "Detach with Love", "My Happiness is My Responsibility", "Worry is a terrible waste of time" and of course, "Let Go and Let God".

The reason these sayings are repeated over and over again is because they are true, and have helped so many! This is because these are not just platitudes, but can be the key to our Recovery.

It is true that we are powerless in the face of another's addiction! No matter how hard we try, or how much love and compassion we show to the Addict, or how much of ourselves we sacrifice for them, there is nothing we can do to 'cure' an Addict!

This truth is horribly frustrating and sad, but it leaves us with no other choice except to take care of ourselves!

While logic tells us that we are powerless in the face of another person's Addiction, our hearts tell us differently, and these slogans are more easily said than done! It is very difficult to 'let go' of someone we care about, who is in trouble! Of course, we will want to help them, even if they say they don't need our help! Just walking away just feels counter-intuitive, as if we are giving up on them!

As those who are close to an Addict, we are prone to being hard on ourselves! We often blame ourselves for things that are not our fault: like not being able to let go of the Addict in our lives. However, this is nothing to be ashamed of, it is a sign of our caring.

Letting go of an active Addict can feel cruel, like if we watched a dog, who fell through the ice, struggling to save itself, and we just turned away saying "The dog has got to find its own way out"! However, this is the way it is with Addiction, it does not make sense! How could a disease that tells those suffering from it that they don't have a disease, and instead drives them to self-destruction, make any sense? But that is how it works, as it is up to the Addict to find their own way out, by realizing there is a problem and asking for the help they need! It is once that help is sought and accepted that Recovery can begin!

Just as a person in Recovery has to take things one day at a time, we too need to practice our Recovery on a daily basis, but because we are human, this is something we cannot do on our own, we need help! We need the help of others in Recovery to keep on track. We need help handling the stress and frustration that comes from having an Addict in our lives, and we need help to learn how to forgive ourselves when that stress gets too much for us, and fall back into OUR part of the disease of Addiction.

With the help of others, who join us on our difficult journey, we can learn how to face the challenges of having an Addict in our lives, and practice letting go, so we can focus on ourselves. Once we are able to practice letting go, we can break free from our co-dependency and see the truth of the slogan: "My Happiness is My Responsibility", and the joy of knowing, we do not have to meet this responsibility alone!

12

On The Edge

You know the local police by their first names, perhaps they've been in your house more often than some of your friends.

You jump when the phone rings, worry about what you will find when you get home from work or when you wake up in the morning. Will there be chaos, tragedy, an ambulance or a police car? You may watch and wait for familiar headlights, the sound of a car door closing, or you may wonder if you will get woken up in the middle of the night by a knock on the door. There has been shouting and crying and much fear and frustration!

And what is even worse, is that living like this has become the new normal, and you may be used to living on edge!

Even if the Addict in your life has found Sobriety, it is not uncommon find ourselves waiting for the other shoe to fall, for it all to go wrong again. Unanswered texts, late night noises, raised voices and unexpected phone calls or knocks on the door, anything out of the 'ordinary' can revive those old feelings of stress and fear.

We may even feel guilt for not being able to trust again, even though they are working on their Sobriety; however, this guilt is misplaced!

It has been pointed out that many people who have had an Addict in their lives suffer from the symptoms of PTSD...and for good reason, as we have been through a trauma!

We have been put through the wringer by our loved one's substance abuse and our reaction to it, and it takes time to heal. A recovering Addict is encouraged to take their healing one day at a time, so as not to be overwhelmed. This will also work for those of us with an Addict in our lives, whether they are still active or sober, and as with any other recovery, we will need the help of others to find healing.

The help of those who know what it's like to be impacted by the Addiction of another person…to know what it's like to live in fear, frustration, and to experience a mistrust of hope. When we gather together to share our stories, we know that we are not alone, and we are open to put aside our shame so that we can receive the support we need to keep healing…one day at time!

And as we do so, we will find freedom in knowing that we no longer have to live on the edge, but are able to experience the true adventure of living life on life's terms.

13

<u>Detach With Love?</u>

How do we "Detach with Love"?

We detach with love by continuing to show love and compassion to the Addict in our lives, while not accepting the trash they are throwing our way or feeding into their illness. It can be a fine line to walk, as detaching with love does not enable us to 'fix' the Addict, but instead, gives us the room to help ourselves!

Seems so simple...right?

Not really! It is actually very difficult, and even more so when the person abusing drugs and/or alcohol is your child! While it is possible (though not always easy) to end a relationship with a spouse or a partner and detach totally, the connection to our children is something we cannot break, no matter where they go, what they do, or even if we lose touch, they will always be our children.

This is why we can feel so trapped when our children are struggling with Addiction, because there is no way out, and no way to 'fix' our kids either! It is heartbreaking to realize that all the love we show them, the common sense we taught them, and support given to them cannot save them from their affliction. Instead, we can get caught up in it ourselves, with most of our time and energy given to the tragedy that is unfolding right in front of us!

A tragedy we are powerless to stop.

As we get caught up this struggle, our lives can also become chaotic. Home became a scary place, as every shout, every slam, every knock on the door would be a reason for fear! And I would also worry when it got too quiet, wondering if my child was okay or not. It would also follow me to work, as having a cell phone means that there no longer the ability to be 'unavailable'; this has cost many their jobs, including myself.

At times we may be so frustrated, stressed and tired, that we knowingly make bad choices to simply 'keep the peace'. On more than one occasion my child came to me for money or the car, and I simply said "Yes" although it was not a good idea. While I never gave my child the car or money when she was obviously high, I didn't need more than two guesses to figure out what they would be used for!

Looking back now, I can see how foolish I was; however, it is important to note that I was not thinking clearly. I overwhelmed by turmoil, frustration and fear, and it seemed easier just to give in and get her out of the house, so I could find a few moments of quiet! Of course, that did not work either, as I wound up spending the whole time worried about her and whether she make it home safe? Would I be chatting with Law Enforcement before the night was over, spending time in an ER, or making arrangements for a funeral?

Every time the lights appeared in the back alley and turned into our driveway, there was relief, and when the Police did come I was often glad they were there to help control a situation where I had no control.

It is true that that as a co-dependent parent, I was nearly as sick as my child. It led me to let people into my home who had no business being there, I allowed behavior that was unacceptable to me, gave rides to uncertain places, and lead me look the other way when faced with shady activities.

I think it would be difficult for any parent not to be co-dependent. It is close to impossible to truly detach with love while watching our child sinking beneath the waves, and all we can do is tell them we love them and turn away. It seems cruel, but if you throw someone a life preserver over and over, and they still push it away, there is not much else we can do. Instead, we need to take care of ourselves as best we can, which is why beating ourselves up for mistakes made is a waste of time and energy.

That said, it is not healthy to continue to simply maintain and survive, because sooner or later the codependent appeasement stops working. Just as with an Addict, it is only when we are able face our problems head on, and admit we need help that we can begin to heal!

And just as with an Addict, we sometimes have to hit (a) bottom before we finally admit we need to do things differently.

When the stress contributed to losing a good job, my car was driven into a ditch and totaled, and I realized that the police in had been in my house more than many of my friends, I finally had to accept that I could not handle this alone. That was when I reached out to others, who had faced similar challenges, and with their help I began to practice detaching with love. Although I did not do it very well at first, just practicing it gave me some relief. In time, I got better at detaching, but it will remain a case of progress and not perfection! However, practicing is good thing, because practice is how we get better at anything. The important thing is the we continue to move forward, and not get stuck in guilt when we take a step backwards, as detaching from our children is not easy.

This is why it is so important that we do not try to face these challenges alone, we will need help, especially from those who have been where we are! Because these people know our struggle there is no reason to feel shame when sharing our stories with them, and this opens the way to healing. For when we put aside the stigma surrounding Addiction and share our stories, we also share hope...something that can be hard to find when our children or loved ones are struggling with Addiction.

It is this hope that can help us and our families to heal, for when we help each other, we can gain the strength and support needed to begin to escape the trap of Addiction. This will free us to face whatever comes next, whether it is grief, sobriety or more of the same.

And our ultimate hope is in knowing that we do not face these challenges alone!

14

Keeping Focus

When we have an active Addict in our lives, it can seem as if it their Addiction can take up every waking moment! We can find ourselves constantly worried about the Addict, will they live or die…will we find them overdosed and unresponsive, when will the Police knock on the door again?

We question whether or not we are handling their Addiction the right way (as if there is a right way), and not enabling them? If the Addict is in our home, we consider kicking them out…but find we do not have the heart for it because we love them and do not know if they will survive!

All these questions leave us confused and uncertain of where to go or what to do next!

Of course, the biggest questions are why can't we help them, and why can't they see what they are doing to themselves…or to us?

This is followed by beating ourselves up with guilt: why didn't we do a better job, why was our caring not enough? And then, we may be troubled by another thought…the wish that this nightmare of Addiction would just be over, one way or another, and that we would all be at peace!

It may seem extreme, but it is natural to want those we care about to be freed from their pain, and for ourselves to be relieved from our own worry and suffering.

Life with an Addict means frustration and stress, and even we may even find ourselves grieving for someone who is still clinging onto life. When we talk to others about our struggles, the conversation often boils down to complaining and venting. Not that venting is a bad thing, it can be a good way of coping with what we are powerless over!

However, when our focus in only on the Addict, we are missing a big part of our own healing: taking care of ourselves, regardless of what happens with the Addict.

Focusing in ourselves is not an easy to do, as the Addict in our life tends to draw all of our attention, leading us to put aside our own needs! It's as if a tornado is tearing apart your neighbor's house, while yours is on fire! There is nothing you can do about the tornado next door, except to get caught up in it, while your own house burns; however, if you can stop and put out the fire and save your own home, you will have a safe place to heal. And you will have a space to offer to any of your neighbors who need a place to stay!

In short, while we want to help those in our lives who are struggling with Addiction, or any other illness, we will not be of no help to anyone if we do not take care of ourselves first!

Keeping the focus on ourselves is to accept that we are powerless to 'fix' the Addict in our lives, freeing us to start looking at how we can take care of ourselves, to handle the frustration that we have in our lives, stress caused by the Addict and the many other challenges that life has to offer!

Keeping the focus on ourselves can open new doors of hope for us! Hope that if we take care of ourselves, we can face whatever challenges we face in our lives, no matter what happens with the people in our lives! Even if the Addict does not find Recovery for themselves, we will survive if we practice our own Recovery, from Codependency!

We begin recovering when we admit that we have a problem that we cannot handle on our own, and then by reaching out to others for help, because keeping the focus on ourselves is not the easiest thing for us to do…it takes practice.

When we reach out to others for help, we are breaking our silence and shattering the stigma of addiction to drugs and/or alcohol, and when we do this, we open ourselves to getting the help to we need in order to heal, and to know that we will be okay no matter where life takes us!

15

<u>Breaking the Stigma</u>

It is not something you want everyone to know about, usually it is kept 'private' a secret that should not be shared.

When we have someone in our lives who struggles with the disease of Addiction, it is understandable that we would want to keep this to ourselves. Having an Addict in our lives can leave us feeling ashamed as well as frustrated, and alone. It often feels as if no one else can understand what we are going through…that we would be judged harshly, by those with 'normal' lives.

The stigma of Addiction is strong, but the shame is not a requirement. The truth is that even those with nice 'normal' lives have their own struggles, and living with Addiction is more the 'norm' than the exception. Most of us know someone who is struggling, it could be a friend, a co-worker, or a family member, or maybe all of the above.

It is this shame and embarrassment that can kill us, and I don't mean just the Addict, because the stress and despair of having an active Addict in our lives can also cause great harm. It can make us sick, can cause high blood pressure, heart disease and depression!

When I had an active Addict in my life, I often had panic attacks, and there were times when I would want to simply get in the car and drive away and never look back!

But I did not go, because I knew that leaving would be wrong.

What I did do was fall into a depression. I wanted to help the Addict, to make it all better, but that does not work unless the Addict wants the help, and this person did not. However, I did need help, as I could not live that way any longer.

The first step in getting help was to swallowed my pride, to look beyond the stigma and to ask for help by reaching out to others. This is how I began to heal. It wasn't always an easy journey, often it was two steps forward and one back. Funny thing is, that as I got better, my home became less chaotic and the Addict started making better choices, moving toward Recovery.

Healing takes time, as it took time to get off track, and it can be frustrating. Even though we are getting healthier, there is no guarantee that the Addict will also find Recovery. It is good to remember that our Recovery is for us, for our own healing, to ensure that we will be okay no matter what else happens.

This is why it helps to connect with those who know what it is like to live with the stress, frustration and pain of having an Addict in their lives. Through this connection, the sharing of our experiences and support, we are able to see that we are not alone, that there is help within reach!

It has been said that we are as sick as our secrets, but when we break the stigma, we can find the freedom to tell our stories, and bring the truth into the bright sunlight of hope.

16

<u>Tending to Ourselves</u>

When we see someone who is drowning, it is natural to want to jump into the water to save them. Unfortunately, this does not always work out well, as sometimes instead of saving another, we are pulled in ourselves!

Up until the middle of the last century, many of the bridges in New York City had Bridge Tenders. These men would manually raise and lower the drawbridges, for the ships that were traveling up and down the river. On one warm June day, in 1943, one of these Bridge Tenders heard shouts coming from the water! Looking over, he saw that two little girls had fallen into the river and were being swept downstream! Without a thought for himself, the Bridge Tender dove into the water to save them! Sadly, the current was too much him and all three of the people drowned!

The Bridge Tender was brave and thought he was doing the right thing. He was hailed as a hero, and he was; however, all of his valiant effort was in vain. In all likelihood, the girls never had a chance, but the Bridge Tender still had to try! However, if he had taken a moment to call for help, the Bridge Tender might have been able to go home to his family that evening. The Bridge Tender could have tied a rope around his waist and had the other person hold on to the rope, so that he could have been pulled back up on shore rather than being washed downstream to his death!

Just as with the Bridge Tender, there are times when we too will want to jump into the deep water to try to save the Addict/Alcoholic in our lives, before he or she is lost to the current. This is a natural reaction, but it is always best to have some help…because there are times when the Addict/Alcoholic cannot be saved, and we need to do all we can to avoid being pulled under as well!

It can be hard to accept that when we are caught up in Addiction, we can only save ourselves from the current, and even this will take help, as we will need someone to hold onto our lifeline, so that we are not washed away! And there are those who are ready to offer that help and compassion to us when faced with those things we do not want to face, when we too feel as if we are in danger of drowning!

These are the people who know what it is like to have an Addict in their lives and have learned ways to cope with the many challenges of living with this disease. Together, we can help to keep each other afloat so that we can get safely ashore.

These lessons learned together, will enable us to help others, as we all trudge this road of happy destiny, which is life!

17

<u>Reaching Out</u>

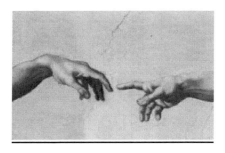

I stepped over him as he lay on the floor of the ferry terminal, not paying him any attention, until he said my name!

I was used to seeing the homeless sleeping in the terminal building. There were shops that sold pastries and coffee, and there was even a McDonald's in the building, which meant that there were dumpsters to dive for food. In addition, some of the commuters were share what they had with the homeless, from food to old coats. There was also a Police sub-station there, so it was a fairly safe place to stay on a cold or rainy night.

The homeless were just a part of our everyday life in New York City, and I learned to ignore them; however, this time it was different. When he said my name and reached out to me, I looked down at him and I saw a familiar face!

He was a friend of a relative. I met him when I was a kid, when the two of them were on the same softball team, but I had not seen him for many years and was surprised he recognized me at all. I knew he had been struggling with both drugs and alcohol for a long time, but I was still upsetting to see him lying there on the floor, filthy, drunk, and alone! I spoke to him briefly and asked if he needed anything (because I didn't know what else to say) but he just told me he was "...doing okay" gave me a (mostly) toothless grin, and that was it. I knew he wasn't doing okay, but also knew that I couldn't do anything about it, and that I had to get to work, so I said "good bye" and ran for the ferry!

I continued to run into him over the next few months. It was winter, which probably kept him indoors, and sometimes I gave him a bagel, coffee or juice, and we talked a little. During the course of these conversations I learned some of his story. He told me of years spent struggling with alcohol, heroin and other drugs, which left him alone, homeless and feeling trapped. I also shared some of my own story, and as I talked with him, I was reminded of what a gift it is to be Sober!

The sad truth is that many people who are addicted to drugs and/or alcohol do not always find Sobriety; however, that does not mean that they die right away either. Instead, they simply subsist day after day, living a horrible 'winding down' life, as their disease takes everything away from them!

Leaving them like my friend: lost, alone, homeless and hopeless.

This also means that the people in their lives have to live with the frustration, worry and fear that comes along with this disease! Having an Addict in your life, is like being stuck in a nightmare, where there are no good solutions, no clear direction...we simply have find a way to cope with it a day at a time! At times we feel guilty because we just want it over, while knowing that whatever ending that comes will may not be a happy one.

Yet there IS always hope, as I have seen people literally pulled up from the gutter and given the help they needed to get Sober and rebuild their lives. I have known many people who struggled to find Recovery for many years, going in and out of active Addiction, who have now been able to find long-term Sobriety.

Many people who have been touched by the Addiction of others, have learned the practice of letting go, and have been able to move on with their lives, rejecting the disease, while still holding the Addict close to their hearts.

This remains a case of progress and not perfection, but we do not practice alone, as any Recovery happens with the help of others, usually those who have been where we are, and who know the difficulty of the journey, the heart-break of failure, and the joy of living free from the prison of Addiction!

As for my friend, his journey is over and he is finally at peace. As far as I know, in the end he had nothing and no one, as he lay on the floor of the ferry terminal in Staten Island, unaware that help was all around him...all he needed was to be able to take one of the many hands that reached out to help him.

And Recovery is just that easy for all of us; however, accepting the hand of help can often be difficult, although when we do, we can find ourselves being pulled out of the darkness of frustration and despair and into the light of hope.

18

Children Suffer Too

My biological mother suffered from Mental Illness, and self-medicated with drugs and alcohol. When I met my biological father, when I was an adult, he told me that this woman, who eventually died of an overdose, was responsible for the abuse that led the neighbors to call the Police, who removed from the home when I was 6 months old. However, I suspect that he also played a role in my abuse, as it would not surprise me to learn that he too had Substance Abuse issues.

I was lucky, as after a lengthy stay in the hospital, I was placed in Foster Care and later adopted, into a good and loving family. *They may not have been perfect, but they were perfect for me.*

However, as an infant, I had no choice in the matter. There was no way for me to detach from my parents, who I relied on for everything! I could not just pack up and leave, and could not call authorities, it is only by God's Grace that I survived!

When discussing the impact of Addiction to drugs and/or alcohol, it is easy to overlook the most innocent victims of this disease: children! Just like in my case, these kids usually have no good or bad options in the face of a parent or guardian who is struggling with Addiction. They are simply stuck!

While Child Abuse is a serious issue that often arises with Addicted parents, it is not the only one. Children can also experience neglect, disregard and malnutrition as much of the food budget is spent on the needs of Addiction. Many teachers have reported that children in elementary and middle school grades are coming to school hungry, angry, bruised, dirty and stressed out!

Then, we have the sad reality that many of these children are losing their parents to incarcerations and overdose.

This is another example of how active Addiction to drugs and/or alcohol can have a far-reaching impact, often in ways that would not be immediately obvious. Not only does it affect the children of Addicts, but also teachers, other students, grandparents, and the extended family!

So, what can we do about it?

We can pay attention to the children in our lives, and if we suspect that there is a problem, rather than dismiss it as an overreaction, we can ask questions (noting that may not always get the truth and offer to help. We can listen, show concern and offer support. We can also help by getting the appropriate people involved: teachers, ministers, police, etc. It is understood that some may feel uncomfortable 'stirring the pot' so to speak, but if a child is at risk, it is important to for them to get the help they need.

We can also help by reaching out with compassion and understanding, while showing consistency and setting appropriate boundaries, which are often lacking in the lives of children with Addicted parents (and in the lives of their parents)! Sometimes, just having a listening ear and showing kindness can open the door to help.

And if help is accepted and Recovery is found, the support of others will be crucial for the establishment of a new and more healthy life for children and their parents, as Sobriety is not always easy, for the Addict or for those in their lives...especially children, which is why it is good to have an experienced guide...who knows the way.

In sharing this compassion and support, we are offering hope to those who may feel as if hope is out of their reach. This hope can make all the difference in the life of children with Addicted parents

19

On a Clear Lake

I remember being on a lake in Maine, fishing with my father and a couple of my brothers. It was a beautiful day, and the only sound was the water against the boat, and the birds calling to each other. Until the silence was broken by the sound of a motorboat coming toward us!

As the boat passed by a few yards away, it disturbed the birds, who flew off in every direction in an effort to get away from the noise. My brother was annoyed, afraid that the fish would be scared away. Then, as the motorboat faded into the distance, we were hit by the wake, which rocked the boat, and one of my brothers almost fell in, but my father caught him in time.

The people in the motorboat never gave us a single thought, they were simply having fun and enjoying the day. It was nothing personal, yet they disturbed the birds, the fish, and rocked our boat!

This is what can be like to have an Addict/Alcoholic in our lives. For the most part, they do not mean us harm, nor do they realize that they are hurting anyone other than themselves. They do not see the impact that their behavior has on all those around them! When an Addict overdoses, or Alcoholic drives drunk, the lives of innocent people are put at risk, as are those of first responders. These events also have an impact on doctors and nurses, and the community at large.

And we cannot forget the impact on families and friends, who have to live with worry and frustration, filled with fear, or have to face a terrible loss!

The wake left behind by an Addict/Alcoholic can be devastating and touches more lives than the Addict could ever imagine! Unfortunately, there is not much we can do, but to ride out the waves, and to hold on tightly to each other, to ensure that we are not thrown out of the boat ourselves!

I wish there were easy answers, but all I can offer is the assurance that we are not alone and never far from hope as long as we have each other to rely upon for support, people who are willing to help because they too have faced the same waves and managed to thrive!

20

Hope is Like a Jumping Fish

It was one of the hardest times of my life. My child was struggling with active Addiction, and I was out of work, out of money and almost out of hope. It was one of those times in life when it seemed like all the news was bad…and the hits just kept on coming!

When I found myself overwhelmed with stress and frustration, and could no longer stand to be at home, I would get out and go the local lake where I would hike one of the trails along the shore, soaking in the sunshine and enjoying the green trees. It helped to be away from home, with my phone off, where I could find some comfort.

I remember one summer afternoon, I was looking out over the water, in hopes of finding some peace. I enjoyed the sounds of the birds, the leaves rustling in the breeze, and water lapping on the shore. The sun was shining on the surface of the water, and I could see the rocks and silt that covered bottom of the lake. As I stood there lost in thought watching the water I began to pray.
I prayed for relief from my stress, for help, for hope, and I prayed for my child. Talking to God, I said (half in jest) that if I saw a fish in the water I would know that there was hope. At that very moment, I heard a fish jump and saw several small fish in the shallow water in front of me, where there had been none a few seconds before!

I have felt jealous when some friends speak of having a "God moment", wondering why I cannot have those. However, seeing these fish, just as I was praying for hope, certainly could qualify as one of these moments; but still I can be a cynic, and I have trouble believing that I could have a "God moment" *those happen to other people.*

While I was moved by the sight of the fish, I found it easier to tell myself that they more of a coincidence, than a sign from God.

It is normal to have doubts, in fact some would say that wrestling with our doubts helps our faith to grow, as it leads us to examine and refresh our beliefs; and I still had doubts! It was hard for me to accept that those fish were part of a "God moment". This doubt came in spite of the fact that I have written a lot about having faith in the face of trials, and the power of hope found in God's grace. I believe in the power of faith, and in the imminent presence of God in the world. I have shared this belief with others to give them support during their own times of trouble and loss, so I ask myself, why is it hard for me to believe that God is present for me?

At that time, I was not feeling very good about myself, as my child sank deeper Addiction and I was powerless to stop it. I felt like a failure as a parent, especially since I was Sober myself but still could not FIX her! I blamed myself for the trouble and it often seemed like there was no hope…at least not for me.

Then, I saw that jumping fish, and began to consider the possibility that there was hope for my child, and even…for me!

I would like to say that things got better right away, but they did not. We had another year and a half of turmoil before things finally began to turn around and improve. However, my outlook did begin to get brighter, as I tried to put more energy into taking care of myself, by reaching out for help. This support allowed me to face the continuing challenges of living with an active Addict, and gave me the tools I needed to keep moving forward if only one step at a time.

That jumping fish helped me to stop and refocus on myself, and reminded me that to see evidence of God's grace, all I have to do is look around me! When I do, I can see that this grace has been with me my whole life. For instance, although I was abused as an infant, I was rescued by an observant doctor and later adopted into a good family. I see God's grace in the fact that I have been able to overcome a learning disability and earn a Master's Degree in Divinity; and in the gift of being able to be a single father, without messing things up too badly, helping her through the milestones and pains of growing up. God's grace is evident in my sobriety, which I have been able to hold onto despite many challenges. It is also present in all those people who have helped me face life on life's terms at times when it felt like I could not do it alone.

Just the fact that I lived to my first birthday, can walk across a room unaided, and can still think clearly is a sign of that grace.

It was God's grace that my daughter got Sober, just when I was starting to think I was going to lose her. Just as it is present in the support given to those whose stories did not have such a positive ending.

Yet, despite the evidence it is still sometimes hard for me to see that God's grace is really for me, somehow, I do not feel worthy…but isn't that the whole point? None of us can earn the grace of God, and that is why it is a good thing that God's grace and love is given to us a free gift! I believe that we are all surrounded by God's grace, that we are immersed in it, and that all we need to do is just breathe it in!

This is what gives us carries us through the darkest days of our lives, when we are feeling frustrated, powerless, and alone. It is knowing that we are surrounded by love and support that reminds us that we are not alone, that hope is never out of reach…sometimes all it takes to find this hope is the sight of a jumping fish!

Part Three:

Recovery: An On-going Event

There Ain't No Cure, But There is Hope

The First Section

Early Recovery

This Changes Everything

What to (Possibly) Expect from Early Recovery

A brief overview.

In the pages to follow, I will share with you what I have learned as a person in Recovery and as someone who has had a spouse and child both struggling with Addiction. However, it should be noted that when it comes to Addiction, every situation is different as we all have our own stories to live! My intention is to give those impacted by Addiction an idea of what they may expect as they start out on the road of Recovery, for getting Sober, just like being in active Addiction, impacts all those in an Addict's life. This means we all need healing!

However, before the healing can begin, we will need to face the roadblocks that can get in the way of Recovery, such as the stigma of Addiction that can cause shame, and the fear that it will just be too hard, that we won't be able to do it (so why even try?). This can be a real problem, as one of the biggest roadblocks we face is that we (the Addict and the Codependent) will often look for any excuse NOT to change!

This brings up another good point (now this is only my opinion): that labels are often just that, an easy way to make an identification. For example, being called an "Addict" is not a bad thing, it is just a fact of life. An Addict is the victim of an illness, no matter what the Addiction is; however, for our purposes, we will stick with those who are Addicted to drugs and/or alcohol. Another label which has been unjustly stigmatized is "Codependent", usually this includes family, partners/spouses, and friends. While Codependency can be damaging, it is often unavoidable, as it is part of being a caring and compassionate human being. Of course, we do not want to see our loved ones suffering from this horrible disease, unfortunately, despite all of our efforts to save those we care about, very little has proven to be helpful! Instead, the Codependent can find themselves suffering from symptoms of

PTSD as they become overwhelmed by stress and frustration. While we may know that the only person we can save are ourselves, our love and decency continue to drive us to do all we can to save the Addict.

It is important to remember that Recovery from Addiction and from Codependency is an on-going process, one that is never 'finished' but that we practice every day!

So... let's begin.

<u>The Decision</u>:

Getting Sober can be a tough decision to make. First the Addict has to admit that there is a problem, and that they cannot "handle it" alone! Initially, many Addicts think that they can take care of the problem themselves, but this is seldom successful. I quit drinking and drugging several times, but I would also go back to it. I always found a reason to pick up again:

- Since I was able to 'quit' for a few days or weeks, then I must not have a problem after all.
    - I can handle it/quit any time I want.
- I'm an adult, so why not have a few drinks, tokes or snorts?
- I just felt like it.
    - I had a bad day.
    - I had a good day.
    - I was with friends.
    - I was alone.
    - I was bored.
    - Etc.

The cycle continued until I was finally able to admit that I had a problem and could not face it alone. I did not come to this admission alone, I had people in my life, some already in Recovery, who lead me to the decision to finally embrace Sobriety...instead of just talk about it.

While I know some who have managed to stay Dry for years solely through will-power, I am not one of those people. And many of these people wound up falling into their Addiction again, or they became bitter and unhappy human beings!

If you have an Addict in your life you may have heard many promises to get Sober, only to see them quickly forgotten. Therefore, it can be difficult to feel hopeful when once again you hear an Addict say that they will change!

Trust is always an issue with active Addicts, as they are not known for telling the truth or for following through on promises! This would be a good time to remember that we have no control over another person's behavior, no matter how much we love them, or what sacrifices we make for them. It is not that this love is without value, it is just that Addiction is a very powerful disease.

Just the fact that Sobriety is mentioned is a good sign, and if it does not happen this time, the day may come when the Addict in your life really does want help, but it has to be their decision, we can't push them into it...this is why I am not a fan of Interventions, but I am not always right, and I do see how it could push someone who is 'on the fence' to get help!

For our purposes we will assume that the Addict in your life has made the decision to get Sober, and has asked you for help. In this case it is good to act quickly, before the Addict starts to detox, and changes their mind, just to feel right again!

But if this time comes, what do we do, how do we get them the help they need and want? While I do not have all the answers, I have experienced many aspects of Addiction and Recovery, and I hope what follows will help.

Detox:

Whether the drug is heroin, meth, crack, alcohol or some other substance, a medically supervised detox is strongly recommended. Detoxing can be dangerous, during withdrawal the Addict can become physically ill, sweating, shaking, confused hallucinating, and unable to sleep. In some cases, the Addict can go into shock. If not managed properly, detoxing can kill (i.e. Amy Winehouse). Many rehabs offer detox as part of their treatment, if this is not available, or there is a long wait for a bed, then the ER can be an option if things start to go badly (and they will)! If possible, find a hospital with a Psychiatric ER, an on-site Detox or Behavioral Health program.

Treatment:

If the Addict goes to the ER for detox, the hospital can help with finding treatment as most have social workers or Behavioral Health professionals who can provide direction. You can also use the internet/social media to search for community groups, churches and outreach centers, who can provide referrals and assistance. Some of these groups may even be able to offer tips on financial assistance/scholarships (yes, they do exist) and on finding a bed, which can be a challenge.

Unfortunately, it may take a few days to get placed, especially if the Addict is under the age of 18. If this is the case, see above: it is a suggested that the Addict doesn't detox at home. If he or she has already been through detox, and are waiting for a bed, attendance at a 12-Step or other support group can help get through the gap.

I believe it is crucial for the Addict participate in the process, because it is important for he or she to take responsibility for their recovery and to find a program that will be a good fit for them.

While choices can be limited due to space availability and finances, it is still possible to shop around. As with any other service, many rehabs are rated on-line, and you can ask for help from family, friends and professionals, especially if they have experience with this process, which will make them a source of good advice.

There are rehabs in Florida, and these can be a good choice for some, as they often have better bed availability due to the number of facilities in that area. In addition, in some cases it can be a good thing to get the addict away from home, making it more difficult to simply leave when they start to feel better (which happens often), it can also help to keep them away from bad influences that could cause them to lose focus! These facts can make going away for rehab more attractive; however, I would suggest that both you and the Addict give this option serious consideration, as there are benefits to receiving treatment closer to home.

Most rehabs offer a Family Program, which can be a crucial piece of Recovery for both the Addict and the people in their lives! It is important because just like active Addiction. Recovery has an impact on everyone it touches, both the Addict and those in their lives. The Family Program is an important tool in helping everyone adjust to the changes that are brought on my Sobriety. Unfortunately, if the rehab is hundreds of miles away from the people in the Addict's life, it will be difficult to have their participation, and could cause issues with post-rehab Recovery, when it all becomes real.

It should be noted that some rehabs offer Outpatient Programs, which allows the person in Recovery to stay at home, as well as go to work and/ or school, and take care of other responsibilities. While there are many benefits with going to an Inpatient program, it can also be argued that an Outpatient program allows the Addict to stay connected with their lives. This can avoid both the adjustment to life in a rehab and the awkward transition back to daily life after rehab. Note these are decisions that should be made with the assistance of a professional.

It should be noted that once a rehab is found, and a bed available, it is best to get the Addict situated as quickly as possible, as this time of decision can be a struggle, especially if the Addict is feeling better after detoxing.

Remember, Addiction is a disease that tells Addicts that they do not have a disease, and affects everyone it touches spiritually, emotionally as well as physically...therefore, putting down the drink or drug is only the first step in Recovery.

When packing for rehab it is suggested to keep it simple. Depending upon the policies of the facility, it may be best to leave the cell phone and any electronic devices at home. Pack a toothbrush and other toiletries, but note that any of these (including razors) may be kept by the rehab for use only when necessary, also most places do not allow outside food. Many patients bring cigarettes or vapes, but again, when and where to smoke will be up to the rehab. Clothes should be comfortable, like sweats, jeans and t-shirts, even during the summer it is suggested that one sweatshirt be sent, as detoxing can make some people sensitive to temperature changes (while the worst of the detox often takes a few days, the entire process can take a month or more).

In most cases, you will be able to travel to the rehab with the Addict. Once you get there, he or she will go through the intake process, but after admission, there is usually a 48 to 72-hour period when the Addict will not be able to contact you, this is to give them a chance to adjust.

When you are on your way home from the rehab, you may feel any numbers of emotions, from relief that the person you care about is getting help, to fear that he or she will be calling you for a ride home within hours, or may just leave and disappear. Both of these can happen, but there is nothing we can do about it, except refuse to let the Addict come home, which is not always an easy choice to make.

It is also common to second guess the decision to have the Addict put in rehab, especially if they start pleading not to be left there, promising (once again) that they can change on their own. This is normal behavior for many Addicts, and while the guilt is to be expected, keep in mind it is unnecessary.

The first few days in treatment can be tough on everyone, and can leave us wondering what to do next. Often, if the Addict lived with you, one of your first instincts will be to (literally) clean up their mess! This is not a bad idea, but it is suggested you be careful! Watch for broken glass and used needles, you do not want a cut! Also, be prepared to find some things that you will not like, such as bottles, drugs and paraphernalia. There may also be damage to your home and furnishings, etc. It may be helpful to let these go, considering that the Addict is in rehab, and is doing something positive...and it should not be too much of a surprise that someone now in rehab was doing drugs or drinking to excess. Pointing out the obvious to them usually does not have positive results, so I suggest you just throw this stuff away, and keep cleaning.

However, it is okay to make it clear to the now Recovering person that this behavior will not be accepted in the future.

No matter how bad the space is, it should not take the full 28 days to finish cleaning, which will leave you with plenty of time to focus on your own healing!

Yeah, I know, good luck!

Few of us like to look in the mirror, it is hard enough to deal with the problems of others; however, we cannot 'fix' another person, but we can take care of ourselves.

While the Addict in your life is in rehab, you can attend a support group for families of Addicts/Alcoholics, like Nar-anon or Ala-non, or a community/church based group! These groups will help you to focus on yourself, rather than on the Addict, by providing tools like detaching with love (still loving the Addict, but not making their crap your own).

And, of course, the rehab's Family Program will also be important! This program will help you to understand the basics of Addiction, and its impact on YOUR life! After all, you have been living with the Addiction for a long time, with little relief, and a person cannot endure this stress and frustration without some impact!

The Family Program can also help you to focus on your own healing, and help to smooth the transition from rehab to home, offering ideas for how to manage early Sobriety. For example: the person who comes home from rehab is not always the same person who left, Sobriety can change the whole dynamic in a relationship, and this will take some getting used to. Also, the majority of Addicts will start going to meetings once they come home from rehab, and this can upset some family members or partners. "They weren't home when they were using, and now they are at meetings every night!" This is a valid complaint, but try to remember that meetings are crucial, and it is not uncommon for a newly Sober person to get really enthusiastic about going to meetings, this usually calms down, but it is still so much better than having them in the bar, running down to Kensington, or locked up in their room!

Family Programs are usually held on weekends, when there is also an opportunity to·spend time with the Addict in your life. Another suggestion: try to keep these visits lite, and easy-going. Enjoy each other's company, have lunch (rehab food is usually acceptable) and just let the conversation go where it may...this may not be the time to blame, accuse or to vent our frustrations.

<u>Back to Reality</u>:

When the time comes for the Addict to leave rehab, they may be almost as anxious as they were about going in, they are leaving a relatively safe place, where they finally got Clean and Sober, and they are going back into the big world, full of temptations and damage that still needs to be repaired. This may also be a tough time for you, due to the whole 'trust' thing. The suggestion here, is to keep things low-key to give everyone the space they need to adjust to another new situation.

Many will leave rehab and go to a 'Sober-House' where they will be living with other newly Sober people, under some supervision to help them continue their Recovery in the face of the people, places and things that so often throw a newly Sober person off track.

If it is decided that this is a good choice in your case, the suggestion is to work with the rehab to find a good Sober-House, and then do your due-diligence as some of these facilities are more interested in profits than in caring for their residents. Note that many states are imposing new regulations that are designed to ensure that all Sober-Houses are operated in a professional manner.

If they come straight home, it's important to be prepared. This does not necessarily mean cleaning the house of all temptation (though this can't hurt), but that expectations should be kept reasonable. Life will not be all tea and cookies after rehab, as there will be a lot of adjustments to make. Sobriety changes everything, and you may find that the household dynamic has changed as well. The Addict who needed to be treated with kid-gloves, or like a needy child, to the Recovering person who is trying to take responsibility for themselves for the first time in years, and there may be some struggle.

Learning to live Sober can be a struggle. For one, feelings that have been frozen for years suddenly flood the person in Recovery, and they may not know how to handle these emotions, or the challenges of facing life on life's terms.

Once source of strength will be the meetings (12-step or other), along with other events and gatherings related to their Recovery. *Some of these activities will be just for fun, as it helps the Sober person to discover that life in Recovery can still be fun...and it will be nice that they will be able to remember the good time, when it is over.* They may also be going to After-Care, continuing treatment which is usually held in the evenings.

All of these activities can be good for the Recovering Addict, but can cause new concerns for people in their lives...like you, as you may feel upset that although now Sober, you still do not see much of your loved-one. The good news is that people seldom come back from a meeting or After-Care screaming, staggering, or smashing up the furniture...nor will they we stealing things to get money to put in the basket (as no dues or fees are charged)!

It is a process, and in time you will see the changes in them and in yourself. If all goes well, eventually you will stop sniffing their breath, trying to get a look into a pocket, purse or backpack, and will no longer be finding excuses to poke around in their room or looking under the seats of the car!

Trust takes time to rebuild. Therefore, for both you and the Addict, it's a good thing to take it one day at a time, if not a minute at a time. Life will be different, and will not always work out as expected. There will continue to be struggles and may even be some setbacks, but there is always hope! Once an Addict gets a taste of Sobriety, they can seldom go back to their drug or drink of choice without thinking of what they learned in rehab and at any meetings they attended. Relapse does happen, but it is requirement of Recovery, and it does not mean all is lost, as in many cases the Addict will try to get Sober again, but even if he or she doesn't (at least not right away), you can continue to heal, by taking care of yourself.

The main thing to remember post-rehab is that the healing has only just begun. Just because your Addict got Sober and is doing well, doesn't mean that you don't have to worry about your own healing. We all go at our own pace, and it didn't take a month or two to get so far off-track, and the damage won't be repaired that quickly either! 'Patience' is the watch-word for maintaining Recovery, either from Addiction or Codependency!

Whatever happens, it is always best to let the Addict work their own program of Recovery, while you work yours.

Everyone has a different experience with Addiction and Recovery, whether they are Addicts themselves, or have an Addict in their lives. This is why Addiction is often so difficult to understand, even for those of us who have the disease, as it doesn't always make sense and each Addict can affect so many other lives! Therefore, please keep in mind that this "guide" is by no means 100% accurate, but only based on my own experience, shared in hopes of giving you an idea of what you may be facing if the Addict in your life chooses to get Sober.

Finally, remember that there is always hope, even if it sometimes seems to be out of reach...there is hope because we are not alone! Addiction has touched many lives, and if we just put aside the stigma and shame, we will see that for ourselves! When we start talking about the impact of Addiction in our lives, we will find that many people share the same experiences, and can offer us the help and support we need to face all the challenges of living with Addiction and Recovery.

Even the heaviest of burdens is easier to carry, if we carry it together.

2

Take Caution

Early Recovery can be tough time, it is often suggested to avoid major changes and new romantic attachments during the first year, as getting Sober all by itself is a life-changing event! While you may have changed how you live, others have not, and most people do not give a second thought to how Recovery has affected your life.

This does not make them bad people, only human.

It is not up to others to ensure that we maintain our Sobriety, it is up to us to guard our Recovery. Often that is easier said than done, as our disease can sneak up on us.

In light of this truth, to follow are a few suggestions of things to watch for when new (or not so new) in Recovery:

- People, places and things that can tempt us, such as hanging out with the people we used to drink and/or drug with, or getting involved in activities that could lead us right back to our drug of choice.

- When at an event, party or bar:
    - Watch your drink, to ensure you do not pick up the wrong glass; a rum and cola can look just like a plain cola, and so on.
    - It's a good idea to stay away from the bar itself if possible.
    - Also, watch for food cooked with alcohol, it is said that it burns off, and probably does, but sometimes just the taste is enough.

- Most restaurants will let you know if alcohol is included, and some will even make these dishes with a substitute – if possible.
    - Bring a Sober friend, or at least take some phone numbers with you…and used them if needed!
        - It can be difficult to be around people who are drinking/using and not to be tempted.
    - Give yourself a way out, don't get parked-in and make sure anyone who is depending upon you for a ride knows: when it's time to go, it's time to go!

- Take medication strictly as prescribed by the doctor.
    - Make sure the doctor is aware of your history.
    - If they are 'good drugs' have someone else hold onto them.

- Alcohol-free beer is a lie and a trigger. Addiction can and does kill people, this disease is not to be trifled with.
    - The same goes for 'Marijuana Maintenance' this can very risky. While I want to be open-minded about this, i.e. "whatever works" I do not personally believe a person can call themselves 'Sober' while getting high on pot. I have never seen this work well.
        - I have no personal experience with CDB oil, but I would avoid it just on principle. For me, just knowing that it is cannabis would be enough to cause concern.

There are many other things to pay attention to, like caution while traveling (I knew a man who had 20 years Sober, and went to Paris with his wife to celebrate…while there, a waiter put a bottle of wine in front of him, and without thinking…he was back to day 1; however, when I met him he was celebrating his second 20th anniversary).

There is also the issue of going to meetings: this has worked well for me over the last three decades, and I would recommend it to anyone wanting to manage life and stay Sober. However, I understand that this disease affects people in different ways, and that there is more than one road to Recovery. I have known folks who have stayed Sober and happy on their own, and those who got caught up in religion (not a bad thing) and that worked for them…the bottom line is to find a path that works, but to watch out for the pitfalls that can not only trip us up, but also spell our doom!

The most important thing to remember is that no one gets Sober by themselves, we need the help of those around us, other people in Recovery, professionals, friends, and family members. It is good to know that we are not alone as we struggle, nor are we unique, we are one of many, and therein lies our hope.

3

A Life Sentence

When I first got Sober, I was working at the World Trade Center, in Lower Manhattan, this area was also where I did a lot of my drinking. When I quite drinking, I also stopped hanging out with my old running buddies, including a friend that I'd had for years, as this is what I had to do to take care of myself.

One afternoon, while on my lunch break, I ran into this friend, down in the concourse. We talked for a minute and I suggested we get some lunch, which he thought was a great idea. His suggestion was to go to one the bars we used to go to when we worked together, where they offered a "Frank N' Stine" lunch special: two hotdogs and a draft beer for $3.00. I considered this for a moment, as I can be something of a 'people-pleaser' but then suggested we hit the local Burger King instead.

When he asked me why I didn't want to go to the bar, I told him that I was Sober, and didn't feel good about being in a bar, especially one that I used to drink at! He gave me a look that said he didn't quite understand, and said, "I didn't think you were so bad, I drank you under the table a few times...and my drinking isn't a problem! In response, I just looked at him and nodded.

Then, he asked me "How long do you have to do this for, when can you drink again?" I told him, "As long as I want to stay Sober...one day at a time." "So, you can never drink again?" He asked, and then added, "It's like a life sentence!" I thought a moment and then answered, "Well, yes...as opposed to the alternative."

He had no response and we went off to have our lunch.

I did not see him again for almost 9 years, when we reconnected through some mutual friends. I went to visit him on a Saturday afternoon, and found him sitting on a lawn chair in his garage, drinking beer, next to a trash can filled with empties.

He offered me a drink, and I told him I was still Sober, which seemed to surprise him! "You're still doing that, huh?" I told him I was, and then he shook his head and grabbed another beer.

During the visit he was never without a beer in his hand, as he showed me around the house he was fixing up (post-divorce) and we caught up with each other. He seemed to be doing pretty well for himself, better than I was after my own recent divorce, except he did not get to see his child very often, while I was raising mine (as a single parent) and he could not seem to stop drinking.

The second was something I knew well, as that was how I drank: once I got started, I had a lot of trouble stopping! For me, it was like I had turned on a faucet and broke off the handle...there was just no stopping until I ran out or passed out!

Visiting with my friend reminded me of our earlier conversation. While drinking and drugging can completely rule our lives (and could eventually kill us), my Recovery was a Life Sentence, meaning that Sobriety is a sentence for life! This is a sentence I am happy carry out, one day at a time.

I've lost touch with my friend over the years, but hope he is well and happy today! As for myself, I am still carrying out my sentence for life, and it truly is better than the alternative!

Beyond Our Wildest Dreams

Early on in my recovery, I was told that Sobriety will take us "beyond our wildest dreams".

Well, I have pretty wild dreams, and when I heard this I immediately thought of the big house, expensive car, and a beautiful woman on my arm! When I mentioned this to an 'Old-Timer' (someone who has been sober for 20 years or more) nick-named "Davey-Bop" (because he would often exclaim 'Badda-bing, badda-bop!'), he laughed and told me that I misunderstood what that all meant.

He explained that "beyond your wildest dreams" did not mean that we would get everything we ever wanted in life, *as this is not always a good thing,* but that practicing a program of Recovery would enable us to simply be able to live our lives, facing any challenge, while staying sober!

Davey-Bop told me that success in life is not always counted in dollars and cents, especially for a person in Recovery! Our real success in life is just staying sober! This may sound simple: to just not drink a day at a time, but as victims of the disease of Addiction, we are hard-wired to use our drug of choice, especially when we hit rough patches in our lives; therefore, each day a recovering Addict spends sober can be counted as a success!

Even if there is a relapse, this does not mean the end of the world, or that our time Sober was wasted, especially if we can use what we have learned, and the connections we have made, to find our way back to Recovery.

Over the years I have been Sober, I have found that it does take us beyond our wildest dreams, because it gives us the tools to face life on life's terms without running to a drink or drug! These tools include the support of other recovering people, who share their experience, strength and hope with us, letting us know that we are not alone in our struggles!

The most interesting thing is that once sober, the recovering person will find that their wildest dreams have changed! We no longer dream of riches, but instead learn to be grateful for simply being alive, for not being afraid to see a police car in the rearview mirror, reconnecting with family and friends, being able to keep relationships, hold onto jobs, having more money, being healthier, etc. We find that just by maintaining sobriety, doors that were once locked and nailed shut suddenly become open again and new opportunities become available to us!

The gifts of Recovery are not just for those who suffer from the disease of Addiction, it is also for those of us who have an Addict in their lives (yes, I know both sides of this coin). Recovery from Co-dependency is not very different from that of Addiction, as in a sense, we become addicted to the stress, fear and frustration...well 'addicted' may not be the right word, it's more like we get used to the drama, and this can often make us as ill as the Addict.

Just as with the Addict, Recovery for the people in their lives requires having the strength to break the stigma and ask for help, along with the courage to accept that help! We are helped by those who understand, because they have been where we are, and we can help them as well, by sharing our own experience, strength and hope!

Life in Recovery is good; however, to get there we must first take the subjects of Addiction and Co-dependency out of the darkness of stigma, and into the light of hope! When stories of Addiction and its impact are spoken aloud, the disease loses ground, and we find ourselves trudging the road of happy destiny, which is Recovery!

While this journey can be exhausting and frustrating, we do not trudge this road alone, as most people have been touched by Addiction in one way or another...all we need to do is to ask for help.

And this Recovery surely will be beyond your wildest dreams!

5

Just Say 'No'?

The young man had been wandering in the desert for too many days to count.

He was hungry, thirsty, hot, dirty and lonely. He had gone into the wilderness to get some clarity in regard to his life and mission, but all he found was suffering! Although he was man of faith, it is understandable to assume that he may have been questioning the presence of God in his life, and if he was really on the right path.

After all, he was seeking to follow a higher calling, but was literally getting nowhere, becoming lost in the wilderness!

Then, in the midst of a hot, dry afternoon, when he felt like he could go no further, the young man saw another person coming towards him! Could this be someone coming to help him, and give him comfort?

Had his prayers finally been answered?

As the figure drew closer the young man saw that it was a man, a little older than he was, robust, well-fed, and happy! Smiling warmly, the stranger called the young man's name, held his arms out in greeting and said "Why are you out here, torturing yourself like this?" "Trying to get myself together, and to find a deeper connection with God." The young man answered. When he heard this, the stranger's smile was replaced by a look of sincere sympathy, and said "You should just give up this foolishness, a loving God would never ask you suffer so!" Then he put his arm around the young man, and tempted him, not just to test his faith, but to test God's love for him, saying "You are starving needlessly, you know you can change these rocks into bread, so do it already, and let's eat!"

Overwhelmed by weariness and hunger, and perhaps feeling like life was not fair (he had sacrificed so much, and would be called to sacrifice even more, and yet he was left to starve in the desert), we can imagine that the young man was tempted to listen to the kind stranger, and give in to the temptation; it would have made things so much easier for him, and very quickly!

However, he found the strength to 'just say NO' to the temptation, and to continue doing what he knew to be right, although it was the harder road.

What if this was you?

If you were sick and in pain, feeling alone and lost, and someone appeared, offering friendship and comfort, and to relieve your pain, saying all you had to do was to listen to him, and do as he said. Even if that meant doing something you knew was not the best thing for you!

People who are Addicted to drugs and/or alcohol may also find themselves lost and wandering in the wilderness. Plagued with guilt, confusion and pain, feeling estranged from their own lives, and not sure where to turn for help or how to find safety and comfort. Feeling so lost, they are vulnerable to temptation: to go back to the only remaining 'comfort' they know, as a way of getting an escape from their pain!

Those in early Recovery can be especially at risk, as this can be a painful and confusing time, as the world begins to open up again, and their emotions 'defrost'.

When out in the winter without gloves, our hands can grow numb, inured to the cold; however, once we come inside and our hands begin to warm up, they can really hurt before they start to feel better.

It can be the same way for the newly Sober, as they begin to feel things again, and have to face the consequences of their past. They can also become frustrated with the pace of their Recovery, or may begin to believe that they never had a problem in their first place...so why deny themselves?

Some people believe that Addiction is a choice, that the Addict is happiest when in the midst of using their drug of choice; however, the truth is that people in active Addiction often struggle daily with whether or not to take a drink or a drug. Many of these Addicts want to quit, they know it is destroying their lives, but they feel powerless to stop.

This disease does not let go of its victims easily!

Many Addicts start with good intentions to get Sober and stay Sober, but often the temptations are too strong to deny. It would be so much easier to just say "No" if temptation came from a frightening demon, or a scary drug dealer like in the movies; however, as it did with the young man in the desert, temptation often comes from a friendly face!

They can be old friends or family members, people who are trusted, and only want to help their friends feel better, by offering them a drink or a drug! Most of these people do not understand the nature of Addiction! They think it can be cured, or at least managed.

This is why it is so hard for an Addict to "Just say NO!", because often the temptation comes from a warm and inviting place, and is offered out of sincere compassion or friendship.

This is also why it is so important for an Addict to get support from those who understand that this disease does not just go away, but needs to be faced on a daily basis...and that it is best when it is not faced alone! People who have faced the struggle of Addiction themselves, and know what it is like to live Sober, one day at a time, despite the many temptations offered by the big world around us!

The young man in our story managed to turn away from the temptation to take comfort for himself, to end his suffering, as he knew that falling prey to this temptation would not only cost him his soul, but also leave the world a whole lot darker!

In time, the young man found his way back to his friends and family, where they helped him clean-up, fed him, and allowed him to rest and prepare for what was coming next. The road ahead for the young man was full of joy and love, as well as pain, betrayal, and even more temptations...typical life on life's terms stuff! Yet throughout it all, the young man never again felt so alone, and did all he could to give comfort and care to others, giving the gifts of compassion and love!

The same gifts we can share with each other, as many of us have struggled with monsters of our own, and while friendly faces can tempt us, those who have travelled our path, who understand, can give us hope...born of knowing each other's pain, born of true compassion!

Born of knowing that true friends don't tempt us with false promises, but support us as we make our way through life.

The Second Section

Holidays:

How to Keep them Merry

Tis The Season

Partying and the Holidays!

They seem to go hand in hand, at least if you watch TV or indulge in Social Media. The message often seems to be that you are not doing the Holidays right unless you are drinking and drugging! Unfortunately, for those Addicted to drugs and/or alcohol and the people in their lives, this can also make the Holidays a dark season of dread!

Not only can the Holidays be stressful all by themselves, but Recovery is an on-going process, and Addiction can still talk to us, even after years of Sobriety...it can still tell us that we do not have a problem, or that we took things too seriously. That we are 'fine' and not really Addicts after all!

That is why being around drugs and alcohol at a party or a dinner, or having someone we trust put our drug of choice in our face, and tell us that "It will be alright to have just one...it's the Holidays" can be very tempting, as this speaks directly our Addiction.

This is why many in Recovery can feel reluctant to participate in the festivities, for fear of falling prey to this temptation.

These fears can lead us to feel as if the Holidays are a dark time to be endured rather than enjoyed.

However, this is not necessarily true, for it is this season when we celebrate the light that shines during the darkest of times! The light that gives hope to the world.

And there is hope for those who struggle, the hope that is found in the knowledge that we are not alone...no matter what challenge we are facing, there are others who know our pain! People who have made this journey, and are happy to share their experience and, and who know the way to the light.

All we need to do is ask!

When we share this light by helping each other face the challenges of Addiction (or just life itself), it only grows stronger!

As this light grows, so does the promise that we will not only survive the Holidays, but maybe even find ourselves with a reason to celebrate, as the light we share together has the ability to banish the darkness forever.

Just Another Day

I spent the day getting drunk and stoned, just like I spent many of my days back then...

As usual...when I did not have to go to work, I woke up hung-over from the night before and forced myself to roll out of my mattress on the floor, got to my feet and made my way to the kitchen, where I hesitated for a moment, wondering if I should, before grabbing a beer from my mini-fridge. Then I took my breakfast into the living room, turned on the Black & White Sony, and then flopped down on the sofa!

I did not have cable, or a remote so I was stuck watching whatever dreck happened to be on the TV, unless I wanted to make the monumental effort of getting up to change the channel! In truth, I was in such pain that I really didn't care much about what was on any way! This was a good thing as there were only a bunch of sappy, sentimental holiday movies showing...the kind of stuff you might see on Lifetime today!

I had no plans, no one to call and no one was going to call me, because my phone was shut off because I did not have the money to pay my bill. I did not want to go anywhere, but even if I did I was such bad shape that I did not want anyone to see me, nor did I want to interact with another person...it seemed like too much effort!

What I did have was the remains of a case of beer, a full bottle of whiskey that I had gotten as a gift from a client and had managed to make it from my office in Lower Manhattan to my apartment in Bloomfield in one piece (most of the bottles I had gotten as gifts were emptied before I got off the train home)!

I also had about a quarter ounce of weed, a few lines of coke, and some snacks, so I was all set to spend another day isolating and feeling sorry for myself...which came in handy when it came time to justify my drinking! And that is how I spent the day: feeling sorry for myself, while getting high, drunk, and watching bad TV with the shades drawn, afraid to go out (pot was making me very paranoid by this time), and miserable about staying in.

However, it was not just any other day, it was Christmas, 1986!

I didn't have to spend that day alone, I could have gone to see my sister and her family, there was also a girl who would have been happy to come over and spend some time with me...but no, I was determined to crawl into a bottle and stay there.

This is where my drinking and drugging took me! While at first it helped me to get over my awkwardness, allowing me to fit in and not feel so socially awkward, by that sad Christmas Day I preferred to drink and drug alone – there was no one to share with, and not being around anyone else meant it was more difficult to embarrass myself, though it did not stop me from making some really bad choices, some that still have an impact today!

Yet, even though I was miserable and (when I was honest with myself) felt trapped by my Addiction to drugs and alcohol, I could see no other way to live! I actually found myself being afraid of getting Sober because I did not know if I could handle it!

This is a common question asked by people who are thinking about getting Sober: "What will I do without drugs and alcohol, how can I face life Sober?" They will wonder if life could be fun without substances, if they will lose their friends and sink further into loneliness and depression! I wondered about these things myself, despite the fact that I was spending so much of my time drinking and drugging alone in my apartment, with the shades drawn! Life was not fun anymore, and most of my friends were "instant" – just add alcohol.

It was not exactly a dynamic and fulfilling life!

Even meeting and marrying my (now ex) wife did not break the isolation, like I hoped it would. Instead, it was more like two drowning people trying to keep each other afloat than a true relationship! Instead, we wound up isolating together (those who have been through it will understand how an Addict can feel alone even when surrounded by people)! However, it was this doomed relationship that eventually led me to lasting Sobriety!

Once I was Sober, I was able to see just how trapped I had been, especially when I found myself doing more in a morning than I used to do in a week! Recovery freed me from bondage to Addiction, giving me a new freedom and a new hope that I never thought possible while I was in my active Addiction!

And this is the message I would like to share with all those who are still struggling: that life is good Sober! It may not always be easy, but who promised that? What we gain from working a program of Recovery are the tools to help us face any challenge life presents to us without having to fall back into old behaviors, and those same tools can help us to move forward in life! Addicts in Recovery have been able to continue their education, get good jobs, build families, own homes, and most of all, help others!

Today, we no longer need to isolate. There are times when we may choose to be alone, as everyone needs some time to decompress (i.e. chill). The main thing is that we do not have be alone, ever! A connection to another person in Recovery is as close as our phone or computer! When feeling alone, or like the phone weighs 500lbs we can also go to out to a meeting or just spend time with partners, family and friends – people we would not have in our lives if we were not Sober!

Sobriety gives us the opportunity to build strong relationships with all of the people in our lives, and this is one of the biggest gifts of Sobriety: reconnecting! With these people in our lives we know that we never have to be alone again, will never be lost or have to feel isolated again!

These are the people who understand, who accept, and who tell us the truth when we need (not necessarily want) to hear it! Together we can face any challenge life has to offer: work, school, relationships, illness, family trouble, our own doubts, and even the Holidays, one step at a time!

I did not always spend my Christmases drunk, high and alone before I got Sober, but even when I was behaving myself while with family and friends, I felt restricted. I had to be careful not to drink too much, and could not wait to get away from the festivities so I could really get drunk! Having a few beers, a couple of mixed drinks, a few tokes...it all just made me want more, but more meant going further into my illness, and into isolation – even when I wasn't alone, as my active Addiction was a very personal thing.

So is my Recovery, but it is not done in a vacuum.

Just three years after that bleak Christmas alone in my apartment, I spent the day helping to feed people at a twenty-four-hour Alaca-thon, where Sober people came together to help each other through the Holiday, to listen to speakers, have food, share gifts, and just have a good time. This helps for those whose family relationships have yet to be repaired, to give them a place to go; it also helps those of us who will be facing the many challenges that can come from a spending the Holiday with family...just because we get Sober does not mean that everyone in our lives will suddenly become healthier!

Once Sober, it can feel as if the sky's the limit, but often reaching those heights can take time and effort, and if we start comparing ourselves to others, we can wind up disappointed and discouraged! We all progress at our own pace, and if we are trying to keep up with others, we can lose sight of what really matters: that we stay Sober one day at a time! If that's all an Addict ever accomplishes, they are a success! Everything else is gravy!

And we will have a reason to celebrate each day!

3

<u>Amateur Night</u>

I never liked going out on New Year's Eve.

When I was drinking, I thought that there were too many "amateurs" out there who did not know how to drink, while I considered myself to be at a "professional" level! This meant having to deal with a lot of really sloppy and obnoxious drunks in the bar or at a party, I got sloppy and drunk almost every night, these people were not used to it, and did not know how to act (hubris). It wasn't like I could take advantage of the situation to meet women, because just about everyone was coupled up, and for many years I was not!

And to top it off, no matter where I went (party or bar) it was crowded and expensive, as most places jacked-up their prices on New Year's!

Then there was the challenge of driving on that special evening!

Many of these amateurs were out on the roads causing problems! At least I knew how to drive drunk! I knew all the ticks: keeping one eye open when my vision doubled, taking mostly side streets, making sure to avoid toll booths and known speed traps, and even driving straight down the middle line of the road, so I would not run into a ditch!

Which brings me to another problem with being out on New Year's Eve: lots of cops, some of whom may not be very happy about having to work instead of celebrating with family and friends. So, they were even more vigilant that night, which was not good for me, as a drunk driver!

Although I have been Sober for many years, I still don't like to go out on New Year's Eve, for many of the same reasons that I did not like to go out on this night when drinking! I have little tolerance for bad drunks and bad drivers, and while seeing a police car in my rearview mirror no longer bothers me, I would still like to avoid interactions with them *although it can be fun when I pass through a DUI checkpoint, and they ask me "When was your last drink?" and to see the look on their faces when I tell them "1989".*

Even when I was living in Staten Island, and working only a few blocks from Times Square, if I had to work on New Year's Eve, I would get out of Manhattan as quickly as possible once work was finished! While getting on the downtown 1/9 or N/R train, I would see masses of people going uptown, toward the festivities, making me even happier to be heading home and away from the crowds, drunks, and high prices!

Although I have had some adventures on New Year's Eve in the past, including going to parties both drunk and sober, spending time with friends, significant others and my daughter, as well as having a few close calls with law enforcement, I have found it much nicer, safer and cheaper to just stay home where I can turn on the TV and watch the people freezing in Times Square, packed in like sardines, with no access to a bathroom!

Today, I found that a good way to celebrate the holiday is to make a meeting (if possible) and then spend the rest of the evening curled up on a warm sofa with Significant Other, sharing take-out and some fancy sparkling water!

For those unencumbered by a relationship, or just looking for something to do on this festive evening, there are Sober Dances, and many groups hold day-long events, filled with meetings, food and fellowship, ensuring that no one needs to spend their Sober holidays alone.

It is not about getting as intoxicated as possible, nor is it about isolating in loneliness or being anti-social, it is simply about feeling close to those we care about and who care for us, about connecting with who and what are really important in our lives!

The coming of a new year can be a time of reflection as we look back over the years we have seen come and go, *and wonder about how many we have left.* However, instead of ruminating on the past, the coming of the New Year calls us to have hope for the future, and to appreciate we have in this very moment, to be 'right' where we are!

We can pause in whatever we are doing at the turn of the year and take a moment for gratitude, for Sobriety, those we love, and for our lives. This way we can enter this new chapter of life with a positive outlook, which can give us the hope we will need to face the adventures of the coming year...together!

4

Independence Day

Holidays can be tough for Addicts, regardless of whether they are in Recovery or still actively using.

The summer holidays, Memorial Day, Fourth of July, and Labor Day can leave Addicts in an especially precarious position, as these holidays are often celebrated with barbecues, parades, music and fireworks, it is also a time when many let loose, either in backyards, or away at the mountains or the shore, and it can seem as if over indulging with drinking or drugging is not only accepted, but encouraged.

Just watch the commercials that show people out and about having fun while throwing down drinks!

For those who are not afflicted by Addiction, these can be good times without any lasting impact, other than a bad hang-over and some embarrassing stories. However, for Addicts and the people in their lives, these holidays can be devastating!

An active Addict can see these holidays as an opportunity to just go wild without getting a lot of flak for it. They can believe that they are free to do as they please, because they are blending in with everyone else (in their view) who are also getting drunk and high. There is a sense of freedom in being able to just let loose seemingly without consequence...although this freedom is often an illusion, as there are always consequences.

For an Addict who is in Recovery, these holidays can bring temptation, as they may find them themselves in the midst of people, places and things that are triggers for them! They may spend time with friends or family members who don't understand Addiction and believe that the Addict can have "…just a few, it's Fourth of July, and you can't go through the day sober!" (Yes, I have heard this myself.) Because an Addict/Alcoholic is hard-wired to use their drug of choice, this invitation can actually make sense as a justification for using again…just this once! It could even lead them to second guess the decision to get Sober, as questioning whether they really are Addicts, is part of the process.

People in Recovery are advised to avoid any situations that could trigger a relapse; however, when it comes to holidays this is not always practical. There are invitations to family gatherings, barbecues and parties with friends, and opportunities to travel. These events can be fun, and Sobriety does not mean the end of fun.

In these cases, there are certain strategies that we can use to…stay Sober. One is to either have another Recovering person come with us, or at least have their phone numbers, and to be willing to use them! It is also beneficial to honest about your Sobriety. We don't need to hold up any signs, but we also do not need to hide it either, as there is no need for embarrassment or shame. In fact, once they find out that we are in Recovery most 'civilians' will either not know how to respond or be overly congratulatory.

But in the end, it will not really matter to most people (though it would if we got high and obnoxious).

Another suggestion, is to always have an exit strategy, a way to leave quietly and quickly if we get too uncomfortable. This means driving yourself when possible and parking the car where it cannot be blocked, even if that means having to walk a block or two. In addition, it's a good idea to let anyone you came with know about your exit strategy: that when it's time to go, IT'S time to go!

While this may seem rude, it is better to be impolite than drunk, and the truth is that if things are getting that intense no one will notice!

For those of us with an Addict in our lives, these holidays can be a time of uncertainty and worry, as rebuilding trust can be a slow process. We too can have a strategy for facing our fears.

We can talk to the Addict and let them know our concerns, doing our best to not be too harsh, or judgmental. Then, once we have said what we need to say, it is best to let it go, put aside our fears and have faith! Of course, this will not always be easy, it takes a lot of practice. It helps if we follow the same advice given the Addict: to reach out to others who have been where we are and understand our fears! These are the people who can help us to keep faith in ourselves, and keep our hope for those who are Sober, and the support to face the damage caused by those who are not!

The reality is that, all the talking, worry and stress in the world will not stop an Addict from using, so it is best for those with an Addict in our lives to practice taking care of ourselves!

Herein lies our hope: in the support and compassion we share with each other...for whether it is from Addiction or Co-dependency, we do not recover alone, but with the help of those around us. With this help, we can find our independence from the ravages of this disease and rediscover the joy of living.

And life in Recovery is good, as it frees us from the prison of Addiction to really begin to live and face life of life's terms. We will face challenges and temptations (no matter what we are recovering from), but Recovery will give us the tools we need to meet these challenges, learn from them and move on...together. This freedom is more than enough reason to celebrate!

The Third Section

One Day at A Time

Living Life on Life's Terms

1

A Continuing Journey

"You'll never drink again, it's been so long!"

I have been hearing this for years, and I have noticed that many people appear to be unimpressed by long-term Sobriety, as if it is no big deal…or that once we reached the 5 or 10-year mark, our Recovery is locked in place.

The thing is that Addiction is a Rapacious Creditor, one that sits and waits for a weak moment to strike!

It was early 1997, and life was less than joyful. I was recently separated and heading towards divorce, I was also a newly minted single parent, and I was approaching my graduation from Seminary, knowing that I had most likely wasted the past four years and more money than I could every pay back in student loans. On top of all this, I was also still grieving an older brother lost in a car accident!

And I was more than six years Sober.

I was going to meetings several times a week, and often in touch with other members of my 12-Step group; however, I was still depressed, did not get much sleep and was very stressed due to the changes in my life and the responsibilities of being a single parent (not to mention the grief I felt over my personal losses).

On this afternoon I was heading to class, but not feeling it, as I knew I probably would not be able to move forward in my career. As I drove along, miserable and beating myself up for the many mistakes I had made, I decided that I would get good and drunk!

I did everything I had learned to do. I thought it through, and I knew that drinking would not solve any problems and in fact, make things much worse…but in that moment I did not care! All I wanted was to dive into oblivion, just for a little while, and get some relief from the pain.

Logic told me that drinking and drugging no longer brought that escape, that it often made me feel worse. It also told me that it would be a horrible thing to do to my daughter (who was not quite 3), but in this case logic failed me, and I made the choice to go to the closest liquor store, buy a big bottle of whiskey, crawl inside of it, and just go away!

I was bound and determined to just get 'ruined' and I would have succeeded, if I had not read the bumper-sticker on the van in front of me: "AA Motorcycle Repair"! For someone on the verge of drowning and grasping at straws, this was a powerful message! I saw the "AA" and realized I was blocks away from a noon meeting that I went to often and I made myself drive there, still ruminating on a drink.

When I got to the church, I walked to the backroom, where the meeting was held. Still shaken, I sat in one of the folding metal chairs.
The average Sobriety in that room was about 30 years, these guys knew me, and knew that there was something wrong, so when the time came for discussion the chair-person pointed to me!

So, I told the group what was going on with me, how close I had had come to picking up a drink, and how I was saved by a bumper-sticker.

I was kind of hoping for a pat on the back, or at least some words of encouragement; however, all I got was a hard-time! These were tough Old-Timers, and they kicked my ass for even thinking of picking up a drink! One guy turned to me and said "Oh man, my old lady left me but I didn't drink over that mess, I just went out and got myself another one!"

That gave me a good laugh and I began to lighten up, and I realized how foolish I had been, but I was also reminded that this disease of addiction does not just go away. In order to stay Sober, it is important to practice our Recovery, one day at a time.

It may sound difficult but it really is not, as Recovery becomes a part of our lives, and because we have help if we want it...just as I did on that afternoon in 1997.

I could say that today, after almost three decades of Sobriety, that I am no longer bothered by thoughts of a drink, but that would not be true. I can still find myself romancing a drink every now and then, but that's okay, because as an Alcoholic I am hard-wired to drink.

Fortunately, by practicing a program of Recovery, and relying on the support of those around me, I can meet the challenges of life on life's terms and that life is much better Sober.

One day at a time.

2

On a Daily Basis

It's not easy to get sober, as Addicts are hard-wired to use their drug(s) of choice.

It is our fallback, when things go bad, or when they go well, we use our substances in an effort to kill our pain, or to enhance our celebration...any excuse! However, in the end, we always come to the same miserable end of self-loathing, regret and remorse! It is this misery that pushes most Addicts toward Sobriety, when we realize that drugs and alcohol no longer work for us: there is no joy, there is no relief, only the feeling of digging our hole deeper and deeper!

But it is also this misery that can hold us back, as we can become used to feeling this way...it is our dark place, familiar and known.

It is when we get tired of digging, and tired of living in the squalor of our Addiction, that we become more open to the possibility of Sobriety.

Those who choose to get help and embrace Recovery, find out that it is more than just quitting, it is about learning a new way of life, which is not simple! In many movies and TV shows, it seems as if once someone finds Sobriety their lives are wonderful, and they move forward into a bright and shiny future, where they get back the love of their families, jobs, etc.! This can lead some people to believe that the Addict can be 'cured'.

Therefore, it is not uncommon for someone in Recovery to be asked: "How long do you have to stay sober?" As if there was a timeframe for recovery from Addiction. It is not as if these people are being mean, they just don't understand.

The fact is for Recovery to work, it needs to be practiced on a daily basis, because we never stop learning how to live a Sober life, how to face life on life's terms! This is why it is so important for an Addict seeking Sobriety to get involved with a Recovery group, which not only gives us the tools to stay sober, but also gives us the people who can support us in our Recovery, because they have taken this same journey, and therefore understand the challenges we face as we struggle to maintain Sobriety on a daily basis.

It also is suggested that a recovering person stay away from all mind-altering substances. Kicking Heroin, but continuing to drink alcohol is not a recipe for success, neither is giving up booze only to take pills or smoke pot…as one often leads to another! We should also be cautious of any foods that are made with alcohol (I know, it supposedly burns off while cooking, but why play that game?), this includes alcohol-free beer (which is relapse in a bottle).

Addiction is an illness that affects us in body, mind and spirit. This is why people in Recovery are also advised to find the resources needed to deal with the stress, frustration and anger that often comes with life, both in and out of any program.

All of these situations could tempt a Sober person to use again, no matter how long they have been in Recovery, as our disease is always waiting for us to slip up! Addiction is insidious, it comes to us as a friend, promising to solve all of our problems, or at least to help us to forget them for a while! This disease will tell us that we were not "that bad" and that we can handle it, if we just do it a little differently this time!

The truth is, that once an Addict, always an Addict, we can never go back to using successfully…but that does not mean we are doomed to failure! For Sobriety is a journey taken one day, one step at a time, and with the help of others. As difficult as it can be, the journey of Recovery is one that is more than worthwhile, and can be fun!

Those of us who have found Sobriety have traded drunken nights, hangover mornings, and feeling trapped by Addiction, for a new freedom and happiness!

And there is freedom in Recovery, the freedom to rebuild and restore our lives, and the lives of those close to us, because Addiction impacts all those it touches, whether we drink and drug or care about someone who does!

We also find freedom in being able to simply enjoy life, to be present, instead of being insulated from it by our drug of choice. This includes the freedom to be happy, and even have fun again.

Many feel that once they put down their substance that life cannot every be fun again…but instead it opens up doors that there previously unknown.

If you are an Addict, or have one in your life, it helps to remember that while Recovery is not always a smooth journey, it is a rewarding one, and so much better than active Addiction! Often, we just need to have a little patience and understanding of how Addiction and Recovery have impacted all of our lives! And to also remember that none of us are perfect, which is why we need each other so much!

For Recovery is a journey that cannot be taken alone.

3

<u>A Reminder</u>

For many years, I had a bottle of Thunderbird wine on my desk.

Although it was empty, the bottle was full when I first took it from a case in my parents' basement, over 30 years ago.

My parents did not drink a lot, usually a glass of wine with crackers and cheese before bed, and my mother choose Thunderbird because it was cheap, even though we teased her for it, she did not care. When my parents drank it, they would use actually wine glasses, and they would sip it!

When I drank it, I did not use a glass, but slugged it right out of the bottle, like the universe intended!

Although I was an active Alcoholic, and would drink just about anything I could, Thunderbird was still the drink of last resort, when there was nothing else around...it was not that tasty, and if too many bottles disappeared my mother would start asking questions! However, at 1:30am after coming home from my second shift job, it often hit the spot!

I passed many evenings this way, both by myself and with friends. Although when I shared with company, they would get one bottle to split, while I would often have a big quart bottle by myself...not only would my friends think I was being cheap (I was) but, they also wondered how I could drink so much of the sweet, fortified wine.

The bottle I had kept for so long had been emptied on one of these nights, I'm just not sure which one, but it was probably in 1983 or '84! For years, I kept change in it, which I would often shake out to buy more booze, and when the change was gone, I would often look at the bottle and wish it could be magically refilled...but that never happened!

Then, after I got Sober, I kept the bottle as a reminder of where drinking took me. I even added some stickers, with 12-step group sayings, to the bottle. These were given to me by Miss Janie, when I was newly Sober! She was an "old-timer" who handed out stickers and advice to newcomers, as she told us to "keep coming back". Now this bottle also reminds of the Saturday morning meeting at the storefront church in Staten Island.

I used to go to this meeting every week, and would sit up in one of the Deacons' chairs, with my sponsor and his friends. These people had pretty much taken over the meeting, which did not make everyone happy. It was Miss Janie who took me aside one Saturday and told me I needed to sit with her, in the pews, and not up front! She told me to just "...sit and listen, so I could learn something" and also suggested that it might be a good idea if I found another sponsor – turned out she was right about both things!

Keeping this empty bottle was a reminder that the disease of Addiction will never go away, and that even several decades of Sobriety does not make me immune to a relapse! This is a way of 'keeping it green', remembering that as an Alcoholic in Recovery I am only one drink away from my next drunk!

It reminded me that Recovery is not a game, it is deadly serious! If I were to pick up and drink or a drug, there is no guarantee that I would ever be able to put it down again...and this will lead to the loss of so much that matters: family, my relationship with an amazing woman, friends, home, respect, freedom, money, health and even life!

Life is good today, but it is not perfect (and neither am I), and there are many excuses to pick up a substance: work stress, money issues, worries about my daughter, relationship, house, etc., and things just not going the way I want them to; however, there are no good reasons to pick up a drink or a drug.

While, I do not know whatever happened to that empty bottle, I can still picture it, and it still reminds me of what the disease took from me, and that what it can still take from me, should I have that one drink or drug (as there is no such thing as 'just one' for me). It also keeps me grateful for each day that I get the privilege of living Sober...and that I do not have to face it alone!

<u>Rock of Hope</u>

We know that Addiction kills people, and it is not just opioids, people are also dying from prescription drugs, Meth and even alcohol. Sadly, it has become so common to hear of someone who has lost their battle with this disease that we are seldom shocked by the news. Not shocked, but still saddened.

Unless, the person lost was someone close to us, someone we care for and love!

After months or years of living with overwhelming stress, frustration and fear, the worst has happened and those left behind are stunned, grieving, and uncertain of what to do, how to survive this tragedy!

This is why people who have lost someone to Addiction are at risk of Depression, and of falling victim to Addiction themselves. It seems counter-intuitive, as logic says that drinking or drugging is the last thing you would want to do after Addiction has killed someone close to you. However, as this disease often runs through families, it is not surprising that those mourning a loved one may turn to drugs or alcohol to soothe their grief and feelings of guilt for not being able to save the Addict – or guilt over finding themselves relieved that the suffering is finally over.

Unfortunately, many survivors are often left feeling alone in their pain, because they are reluctant to talk about the illness of Addiction, or the impact it has on their lives. Often, they will discuss the related symptoms, such as heart or liver failure, but Addiction is seldom mentioned as a cause of death. This is understandable, as there is still shame surrounding the disease, and an Addict's death is usually painful and slow, making it painful to talk about.

Even in the obituaries and at the funerals, the disease of Addiction is seldom mentioned, usually out of respect for the deceased and in consideration of the survivors. However, this denial can actually cause more pain for those in mourning, as a wise person once said "We are only as sick as our secrets".

The truth is that Addiction is an illness that only grows stronger in the darkness of secrecy and denial. It is a disease that tells its victims that they don't have a problem, which may explain why, on some occasions, the person lost to Addiction is remembered with a toast of their drink or drug of choice...with few seeing the irony.

This can be compared to honoring someone who died of lung cancer by smoking cigarettes in their memory...which is not the most appropriate thing to do.

When an Addict dies from this disease, the truth does not need to be hidden due to unwarranted shame or guilt for not doing enough, *as only the Addict has the power to stop this disease...by first admitting there is a problem, and then asking for help.* For those who find themselves relieved that the suffering is over, and think themselves terrible people, it should be noted that there is nothing wrong with feeling relieved, as it is normal for us to want those we care about to be out of pain, and for ourselves to be free as well!

When shame silences grief, those who have lost someone to addiction are denied a source of strength and comfort. However, once the stigma is broken those who mourn will discover that they are not alone, that there are many who have faced these same struggles, who know the frustration, fear, and tragedy of Addiction.

When we allow ourselves to ask for help, we can gain support and comfort from the experience of those who have walked the same path in life. Together, we can find our way through the darkness of our grief and into light of the hope and healing...so that our lives can go on.

While we may never completely end the disease of Addiction, we can win the battle, one Addict, one family, one community, at a time...together we are stronger than Addiction!

How it Works (for me)

I was handed a joint and a beer when I was 16, and did not put them down for 10 years!

I was on my way to the Washington, DC area, riding in the passenger seat of a 1978 Datsun 280sx, flying down 95 South. I was looking forward to a week away from home and school for Spring break, and the person who handed me the joint and the beer thought he was doing me a favor. What happened was in no way his fault, in fact, if he had known the devastation that this was to wreak on my life, he would have slapped them out of my hands!

Sometime I wonder, had I known what I was getting myself into, would I have just said "No, thank you", or being young and invincible (foolish), would I have thrown caution to the wind, thinking "It couldn't happen to me" and tried it anyway?

Maybe…

That doesn't really matter now, it is what it is…and I believe that I am a better person for having walked through the fire of Addiction, and am grateful that this journey to Sobriety only took me 10 years, many are trapped in their active addictions for much longer, and many will die from it.

Many years ago, when I was new in Recovery, a friend suggested that when I share my story that I start at the very beginning: with my birth, because the story is interesting, and has a definite impact on the course of my life.

I was born into a very dysfunctional family. Meeting my biological father after I was adult and sober, showed me how very fortunate I was for being adopted. He told me a story about what happened to me prior to being taken away by Child Welfare, though I can't say that I trust his version of the events. He blamed my biological mother for it all, saying she had both Behavioral Health and Substance Abuse issues, but he did not unpack these claims, and I did not push.

From what I was told, it was her mental illness and addiction that led to the abuse, which led to a call to the police, who took me to the ER with massive injuries at 6 months of age. Thanks to the intervention of Dr. Henry Kessler, who was working at the hospital where I was taken, I was removed from my abusive parents, and after being treated for my injuries (free of charge), my case was taken over by Newark Child Welfare, who was hoping to place me with a foster or adoptive family, while my medical care continued.

While I won't go into the details of my adoption, I will say that this was the best thing that could have happened for me, as I wound up part of a great family! They were loving, compassionate, and accepting, and there was never any attempt to make me feel as if I did not belong, as if I was different from them.

My parents yelled at me from time to time, and my siblings teased me, and we argued and fought, just like any other family.

Despite meeting my biological father, I always considered my 'adoptive' family to be my REAL family. That said, in spite of the best efforts of my family, I always felt a bit…off. I looked different, with red hair and blue eyes. I hated sports, *probably because I was very awkward and lacked coordination*, and I was a lot younger and sometimes had a different (i.e. unusual) way of looking at things.

Unfortunately, the kids at school were not as kind and accepting as my family, and I was teased for my differences. This was made worse, when I started at a new school, half way through third grade (my previous school not being a good fit with my Dyslexia) and the teacher introduced me to class saying that I had "…a learning disability, but that does not mean he's retarded." Note, this was 1972, a time not as enlightened as today, and of course, all the kids heard was the word "retarded" and this set the stage for the rest of my school career.

Needless to say, by the time I was a teenager, and was taking that ride to DC, I felt that I didn't quite fit in anywhere, though I was most comfortable with my older siblings and their friends. I had tried beer before, and even had a few mixed drinks and wine, but when I took that first hit of the joint and the first swig of beer somewhere on Route 95 South, it was like I found the answer! Here was something I could do, and do well! Here was a way to fit in!

I spent that first week partying all I could. There was no 'ramping up' for me, I went from zero to sixty immediately! I drank beer like it was soda, would smoke-up and then go ride the Metro into DC to wander the museums, and explore the city. Then, on my next to last night, there was a party, but I was hammered before it even started, then I had some harder stuff, and this led to my first black-out. The next day I had my first real hangover! Most people would have quit right then and there, but I could not get enough of it!

That was April, 1979, and for a while, as I finished high school, my Addiction was intermittent, meaning that I did not always have access to pot, pills or booze, but when I did, there was no holding back! Then, in September of 1981, I started college…and the rest of the 1980's is a blur to me!

I do know that my Addiction to drugs and alcohol took me to dangerous places. I often went to the housing projects in Newark, NJ to buy 'supplies' and on one occasion, shots were fired at me. I was never robbed, but to this day, don't know why not. I also went to some after-hours places where I was advised "Not to look at anyone." But did notice a lot of cocaine and other substances, which reminded me of the movie 'Scarface'..

In spite of my Addiction to drugs and alcohol, I was able to hold down several jobs and graduate college, it only took 5 years, but I made it! I spent the summer after graduation basically homeless and broke. Finally, I was able to sell me car to get some cash, and although I had not had been living on peanut butter sandwiches (jelly was too much of a luxury), the first thing I did when I had money was to get beer, not food!

Eventually, I found work on Wall Street, which gave me easy access to drugs, bought in alleys, or in the backrooms of bars, where I was sometimes asked if I had a badge (and searched for one) and only narrowly avoided arrest on several occasions. I endangered my job by doing coke in the bathrooms, and by being obviously drunk while at work. I believe the only thing that saved me there was the fact that it was the 1980's and many of my co-workers and bosses were also drinking their lunches.

By 1990 this leniency had gone away, as companies began to evaluate the impact of active Addiction on their business.

My Addiction also caused me to wake up in strange places, like the floor of the Port Authority, on subway trains in the far reaches of Queens in the early hours of the morning, and with women I did not know. Yes, I had black-outs, and I would not recommend them to anyone, they are not really all that much fun!

It should go without saying, that during my active Addiction I often drove drunk, and it is a miracle that I never had an accident, or killed anyone! On more than one occasion, I had to drive with one eye open, because I was seeing double. There were also trips on the Garden State Parkway in the early hours of the morning, when I had to drive right down the white line in the road, so that I would not go into the woods!

Then there was the time I lost feeling in my legs, while driving drunk and stoned during an ice storm (in a car with bald tires)! Crazy stuff, but I never got a DUI! In fact, the only time I was ever pulled over for DUI was by a cop that I knew! We had actually been drinking in a bar the night before. He knew I was only a few blocks from home, and he cut me a break, and followed me home instead of arresting me. After he watched me get out of my car, he told me that if he saw me driving again that night, he would have no mercy. I listened and avoided the DUI!

I doubt that I would get such a break today.

While my Addiction was active for about 10 years, there were times when I tried to quit on my own. I could stay dry for a few hours, or for a few months (like when I got sick and could not drink for 6 months – but I did smoke plenty of Pot), but I always went back when I started to feel better and was able to convince myself that I wasn't really an Alcoholic, and could 'handle it'.

Ultimately, my Addiction led me to a disastrous marriage, which was really two drowning people who tried to grab on to each other to stay afloat! It didn't end well. However, some good things did come from this marriage. The first is that it led me to get clean and sober, and stay that way! This led to the second amazing thing that came from the marriage: our daughter, who has grown into an amazing person, and who has never seen me drunk!

While I will not go into her story, it was my ex-wife's struggle with Addiction that moved me to get help for myself! After she had a black-out that left her wandering a bad neighborhood (she was rescued by a recovering Alcoholic) and had started treatment, we were advised by a Psychiatrist to both look into giving up drinking, and to maybe give the 12-steps a try. Later, when talking about this with my sister, an RN, she said she thought I had a Cold while my wife had Pneumonia! This gave me pause, as I knew that if a Cold is untreated, it can turn into Pneumonia!

So, in April of 1989, I quit everything, yet again! I was determined this time, after all, I was doing it to support my wife in her recovery! This resolve lasted less than a week!

It was one of the first really nice days of spring, and my manager asked me to take some Financial Securities to a client at 8th and Broadway. I had worked as a Bonded Courier a few years earlier, and was still technically Bonded, which is why I was chosen to make this emergency run. Because it was time sensitive, I took the Subway from the World Trade Center to make the delivery, which went well. For the trip back to the office, I decided to walk, seeing as it was so nice out!

Remember, I had just recently given up drinking…again, but I decided to stop at a small Bodega and get a 'tall-boy' of Miller Lite! I could lie and say that my last drink was an event worthy of police, firefighters and reporters…a story filled with whiskey and depravity, but it was just a Miller Lite, and I didn't even finish it! I drank half of it, and became disgusted with myself, because here I was…drinking once again! In the past, I would have just said "oh well" (or something less 'family friendly') and just kept going, but this time, I did something different and I threw the HALF-FULL can away! So far, I have not touched another drop of alcohol or gotten high since!

Accept for the one time at church, when I accidently got the communion wine instead of the grape juice.

While I may make it sound easy, it was not! I did not go to Rehab, which was just getting to be more popular then, and I did not go to meetings right away! I detoxed on my own, and did not miss a day of work! I was helped by the fact that I had tried to quit a few times already in the previous months, so I had cut down a lot, but still…it was not fun! I had the shakes, sweats and dealt with sleepless nights and bad dreams! I did not say much about it, not even to my wife, I wanted to tough it out on my own. I did drink lots of Coke (the soda) and water, as I did not drink coffee back then, and I ate a lot of snacks, putting on a lot of weight!

I managed to limp through the next 5 months without drinking, though I did take a few of the pills my wife had around…so I was not entirely sober! My wife did not stay entirely sober either, which actually helped me to stay away from the booze myself, as I felt responsible for taking care of her. It was not a fun time for me, and I often caught myself saying that I would try a 12-step group, if I did drink again!

Then, one night, when I picked up my wife from her meeting, I wound up talking to a guy about my own drinking, and how I had been dry for 5 months, and how difficult it was! He told me that there was a better way, and encouraged me to try the 12-step meetings, not to wait until I drank again, as that might be too late!

I thought about it for a few days, and realized that I was in bad shape and so was my marriage, and decided that it was time! So, on a Monday night, September 11, 1989, I dropped my wife off at her meeting and went to another one (as was suggested by my new friend). This other meeting was in the New Dorp section of Staten Island, off of Hylan Blvd, on Greely. As I drove to the meeting, I was still on the fence about whether I really needed to go, looking at the 5 months I had clean, and thinking: "I can do this myself!"

Then, while stopped at a red light, waiting to turn left for the meeting, I heard someone calling to me! On my right, was a young woman who was in business for herself and she was waving a bottle of Jack Daniels and asked me if I wanted a 'date'! I have to admit to being tempted, and thought about turning right. Instead, I made the left turn and went to the meeting!

It was held in small church. Walking up to the door, I stopped and was about to ask a guy smoking a cigarette if I was in the right place, but before I even opened my mouth he just nodded and said "You are in the right place." and he shook my hand as he directed me to the meeting room. Once inside, I sat at an empty table and put my head down. I was nervous and sweating, not sure oand when I looked up, I saw the table was filled with guys, and one of them asked "You're first meeting?" "How could you tell?" I answered, and they all just laughed!

I do not remember much of what was said during the meeting, but I do remember afterward, talking to one of the men at the table, and saying "I'm not sure I belong here, I have been dry for 5 months." Then he asked if I had enjoyed those 5 months, and I told him "Not really." Then he told me something that has stayed with me ever since: "No one comes to these meetings by accident, so if you're here, why not just stay here…instead of trying to come back once you wake up in the gutter again!"

I decided to stay!

I have been Sober since that night. It has not always been easy, but it was easier than having deal with the endless cycle of Addiction, drying out and then Addiction again. Often, during the first few years, I questioned whether or not I really belonged in the meetings, but every time I questioned this, I was reminded of what I was told at that first meeting: "No one comes to these meetings by accident".

With the help of the people in my 12-Step group, I found a reprieve from my Addiction. That said, I have never, and will never consider myself to be cured. I do not believe that it is possible to be cured from Addiction.

Years ago, I knew a guy named Clarence, who was over 30 years Sober, and he would say he never wanted to think he was cured…because if he did, he would probably go out and drink again!

As for me, I believe that if Jesus himself appeared, touched my shoulder and told me I was cured, my reaction would be to put my arm around him, and say "let's go to the bar and try it out!"

This is why, even after decades of Recovery, I still have to pay attention to my disease every day. However, it is not always a struggle, as Recovery gives me the tools to live life one day but it is not always a struggle!

My Recovery has led me to restore relationships with family and friends, including making amends with both of my parents, while they could still understand what I was saying, before being taken by Parkinson's and Alzheimer's.

Recovery has seen me through leaving Wall Street and starting over in Publishing, only to leave New York, and move to Philadelphia, where I earned a Master of Divinity Degree. It also helped me to deal with the failure of that new career to launch after I graduated. Then, when I was hit with Divorce, the loss of my older brother, and becoming a single parent, all at the same time, my program of recovery helped me to meet those challenges as well, without drinking!

But at times it was close!

One day while I was on my way to school in Philadelphia, I got it into my head that I was going to drink! I thought it through (like I was taught to do) and knew that it would not help me, but I was in such pain that all I wanted was that oblivion, not to feel anything for a little while! I actually started looking for a State Liquor Store, when I looked up and saw a bumper sticker on the van in front of me for "AA Motorcycle Repair"! That brought me to my senses and instead of the liquor store, I went to a meeting, put my hand up and got the help that I needed to stay sober!

One of the old-timers said to me: "My old lady left me, and I didn't drink over it…I just went out and found myself another."

My Recovery has also helped me to meet the greatest challenge of my life: raising my daughter from a toddler to an adult, as a single father! Of course, I did not do this alone, I had lots of help from other parents (single and otherwise) who offered me advice, a kick in the butt when needed, and a break every now and then!

Being sober also allowed me to rebuild a relationship with my ex-wife, and this has helped us to offer support to our daughter as she faced her own struggles with Addiction and Recovery and the impact it has had on all of our lives. I was also helped by having been in a 12-step group myself for so long, this gave me an understanding of the disease. Although I still felt guilty about not being able to save my daughter from her own Addiction, I knew that there was nothing I could do to fix her, but I could take care of myself, with the help of the people in my life, both in and out of Recovery.

My experience has taught me that no matter what challenges we face in life a drink or a drug will not give me the solutions. Instead, these challenges must be met head-on, and the good news is that we don't have to face these things alone! No matter what we are going through, someone else has already been through it and understands. All we need is the courage to ask for and then accept the help of others!

This help, and my faith in a Higher Power has kept me Sober for all these years. Recovery has seen me through the loss of people close to me, a failed marriage, failed jobs, failed relationships, serious injuries, and a loss of hope.

As I practice my Sobriety each day, I am reminded that we are all surrounded by hope, and that life, in spite of itself, really is good!

Recovery has been a great gift, which has taken me to places beyond my wildest dreams! No, I never got rich, famous, or successful at business, but my life is richer and fuller today than it ever would have been if I had never gotten sober! It is a gift that I treasure, and guard, one day at a time...with a lot of help.

6

<u>There Are Many Paths to Faith</u>

Like many other towns in the late 60's and early 70's, the town I grew up in was in 'transition'. The tax-base shrank as the wealthier residents moved farther out in the suburbs, away from the more 'urban' areas like Newark and Jersey City. This left our city struggling for funding, which impacted all of the services, from the fire and police (it was not uncommon to see one of the aging squad cars broken-down and smoking), to sanitation and the school system!

During Second grade I was diagnosed with Dyslexia, and while I took special reading classes in public school, my parents decided I would do better in a private school where I could get more attention. After some searching, they settled on a small Christian school, a few towns away, and my public school adventure ended half-way through third grade.

I did not mind, as I was not very happy at public school because it was over-crowded and under-funded and as I was the only kid with red hair and freckles, making me something of a target for bullies. So, I was glad to be moving on, especially to a Christian school, where I assumed the kids would be nicer and it would be like going to Sunday school all week!

I had been brought up as a Lutheran, and had gone to other churches on occasion, and figured they were all pretty much the same. However, it was at this church that I learned that there are a variety of Christians, and we don't all hold the same beliefs.

However, my new school was owned by a Christian Evangelical church. This church believed that God's love and salvation were to be earned by living a good life. They had posters on the walls with a finger pointing up for "One Way" to Jesus (my church taught that it was God who came to us). They were also strong believers in the Rapture, the time when Jesus would return to Earth in all his glory to take the righteous with him to their eternal reward…leaving the 'rest' (non-Christians, those with different lifestyles, drug addicts, etc.) behind to fend for themselves.

The stories we were told did not sound very rapturous to me, instead, they made afraid! These stories made God sound vengeful...and unfair. This eventually led me to question what it really meant to be a Christian. In time, my search for answers led me away from the church, as I sought out different sources of meaning in life...and this, unfortunately, contributed to my fall into Addiction to drugs and alcohol!

However, it also eventually led me to Sobriety.

Throughout the years of active Addiction, while I never lost faith in God, I shied away from religion. I said prayers when I found myself mired in a foxhole of my own making, and the only time I went to church was for funerals, weddings and Baptisms; however, it was while I was attending a Baptism that I heard a sermon that changed my life!

The message was not new to me, but this time I was actually listening! The pastor spoke about God's imminent presence with us, walking with us from the beginning to the end of our journey, supporting us both through the Holy Spirit, and through the people in our lives. He also preached that we are forgiven through no fault of our own, but out of God's love for us! This love is what led Christ to pay for our sins, so that we no longer had to worry about being 'good enough' to earn God's Grace…it is already ours!

Not long after hearing that sermon, I made a commitment to Sobriety and began to attend 12-step meetings.

Throughout the nearly three decades I have been in Recovery, I have run into folks who got Sober by 'finding Jesus' rather than through the 12-steps. They found their strength and support through their church, or through a Christian based Recovery group. Due to my previous experiences with Evangelicals, and the resentments I nurtured, I did not take them seriously and sat back expecting them to fail...some did, some did not, just as with any other program of Recovery.

I realized then, and know now, that this attitude is hypocritical, especially since religion has been very important to my own Sobriety. It brought me back to my own Christian faith, which in turn has helped me to stay Sober in spite of many challenges.

I was especially attracted to the whole idea of 'free grace' as I believe that Sobriety is a free gift, nothing I deserved or could have done on my own!

Yet, I still have an issue with mixing Recovery and Religion – especially Evangelical Christianity, and while I have found my own attitude troubling, I have done my best to ignore it. To just accept it as a character defect.

I was okay with this, until a recent conversation I had with a friend, who is a pastor himself. He asked me why I was so negative on the idea of the Christian approach to Recovery, noting that it has helped many people. I explained that I had seen many people turned away from Recovery by overzealous Christians who told these folks that they had to "...get right with Jesus" or they would be doomed to fall back into Addiction!

I have also heard Christians say that people like Addicts, and those suffering from AIDS deserved to die, because they live ungodly lives.

I also told him that when people are new in Recovery, they are often looking for a reason to go back to their drug of choice, as our disease tells us we do not have a problem! Pushing religion on them would give them a good excuse to run!

My friend chided me for closing my mind to the idea that some people can get Sober by following their Christian beliefs. He pointed out that for some, there is great value in combining religion with Recovery...something I have seen for myself. As he spoke, I felt an argument rising in me, about the damage of Evangelical Christianity, and how (in my view) it pushed Jesus on people...but I thought better of it.

I thought of my niece and her non-denominational church, and how supportive they are of each other, how important they are to her family, and I began to think that there may be something to what my friend was saying to me.

The conversation was short, but meaningful, as it led me to start re-thinking my position on the role of religion in Recovery, as well as the role of my prejudices in my own attitudes. Once again, my friend had reminded me that I did not have all the answers...and was not quite as open-minded as I thought I was.

And I appreciated his openness and honesty!

While many Recovery programs encourage us to find a Higher Power, and to make use of prayer and meditation...this does not mean we need to believe in God, a deity, of follow any formal religion in order to find successful Sobriety. Even the Third Step mentions "God as we understood Him". This Higher Power, can be God, nature, the universe, the Recovery group itself...just any power that is stronger than we are alone!

While practicing a religion may not be a prerequisite for Sobriety, it is often helpful, no matter what faith we follow, whether it is a religion, spirituality or just a belief in a power greater than ourselves, faith is an integral part of Recovery. I know first-hand that religion can give us hope and faith, and access to a supportive community, to a church, which can help us to face the daily challenges of life in Recovery.

Although I am a strong proponent of 12-step groups, I know that there are many ways to get Sober. Just as I believe that God comes to us in ways that we can understand...so too does Recovery, it comes in ways that will work for us. It is not a 'one size fits all' type of thing, and far be it from me to deny a person struggling with Addiction (or the people in their lives) a source of strength and comfort...because they found a different path than I did?

The important thing is that we find something that works for us, and the people who will help us as we journey forward together, facing life on life's terms, in faith!

7

We Also Laugh

A note about Recovery from Addiction:

Many people find it surprising that it is so easy for us to laugh at ourselves!

Both newcomers and visitors to our Recovery meetings don't expect to hear laughter echoing from the backrooms and basements where we hold our gatherings. The perception is that Recovering people are solemn, serious, and don't have much fun…as how much fun can Sobriety really be, how can anyone have fun without drinking or drugging, and facing the wreckage of our lives?

The answer is, a lot!

Recovery has freed us from the dark bars, stuffy apartments where the shades are always drawn, as well as those spaces under highway overpasses and the musty rooms of abandoned buildings where we used to indulge in our drug of choice!

Sobriety breaks the shackles of Addiction, allowing us to enjoy our lives, learn from our mistakes and to laugh at ourselves.

And we tend to laugh a lot, both with each other, and at ourselves!

When together, we'll often tell stories about the stupid things we did when using, things that were not that funny when they happened, but are more humorous now that we are Sober.

For instance, one old timer (someone with over 30 years Sober) told the story of losing his car after a bad night of drinking. This was not an uncommon occurrence, he often 'misplaced' his car after a night of drinking, and usually found it on his front lawn, parked around the corner or still at the bar he had been at the night before because he had walked or gotten a ride in a black-out.

This time, as he wandered the neighborhood in a hang-over daze, he could not find his car anywhere! So, finally, he gave up and called the local precinct! The officers there knew him pretty well, as they were often the ones who gave him a ride home (this was in the 1960's, before the DUI laws became more stringent). The Desk Sergeant told the man that they knew where his car was, and that a patrol car would be over to pick him up shortly.

When the police came, they were laughing, and told him to get into their car. Then they drove him to a spot under the Bayonne Bridge, and there was his car, doors opened and battery dead! That's where the police had found him, passed out in the early hours of the morning, before taking him home!

There are many of these stories, that we tell, not only to make people laugh, but also to remind ourselves of where we were, and where we could be again!

And we also keep ourselves in-line, by laughing at the dumb things we do today, because we do not become beatified simply because we got Sober!

This sense of humor helps us to deal with our pain, it relieves guilt and allows us to let go of regrets…and this frees us to focus on our Recovery and to build new lives. The 12-steps are about clearing away the wreckage of our past, so that we do not fall back into active Addiction brought on by this guilt. Then they teach those in Recovery how to handle…well, Recovery! Living Sober is not always easy, but it is better than living in active Addiction!

Sharing our experience, strength, hope, and our humor with each other makes the road of Recovery smoother, less lonely, and more fun!

The Sober life is full of possibilities we only dreamed of (and some we couldn't imagine) on our barstools, or while we were dipping out somewhere. While we are now able to pursue our dreams, we are not always successful, and we can use humor to face these disappointments as well, making light of our failures, without beating ourselves up – and in sharing these stories, we will find that everyone has failures they have had to face, and learn from, and in our fellowship, there is healing that could never come from the bottom of a bottle, a pipe, pill, powder or syringe.

As we practice Recovery we get the tools needed to stay Sober, to make amends for the wrong we have done, as well as to be better people as we move forward. People in Recovery have raised families, gotten degrees, gone far in sports, business, the arts, and even politics…but most of all, being in Recovery can bring people the hope and the peace of mind that they were looking for during their years of Addiction!

Many who are Sober, find that they do much more in a day now than they used to do in a week, when drunk or high! We have fun by going on vacations (and remembering them), waking up the morning after a celebration and NOT being afraid of what we did the night before, in reconnecting with family and friends, and in getting out into the world and experiencing all it has to offer!

Living Sober takes some work, and calls upon those in Recovery to go against their instincts and face problems in their lives, instead of running away; however, the Sober life is also a good life which gives us the resources to face these challenges, as well as many reasons to laugh, and to experience the joy of living…and there is so much joy in living in spite of this deadly disease!

Best of all, we do not do it alone, but walk (and even laugh) with everyone else who is in Recovery!

8

<u>Take Your Medicine...Carefully</u>

"We are not martyrs"

The speaker was sitting at the front of the room, on a metal folding chair that dated back to the 1950's, behind a rickety wooden table that was probably in the room since the facility opened as a retirement home for old sailors, about 100 years before. A cup of coffee was steaming in front of him as the smokers were anxiously twisting in their seats, waiting for a break...so they could go outside!

We called him" Tommy No Socks" because he never wore socks, and to differentiate him from "Sunshine Tommy" (back then, everyone in 'the program' had a nickname) who was so positive it bordered on annoying!

Anyway, Tommy No Socks was telling his Recovery story, and was talking about his recent hernia surgery.

It was not that he was bragging about it or showing off his scar, but he was sharing about the pain he was in after the operation, and how reluctant he was to take pain meds out of fear that it could cause him to lose hold of his Sobriety.

This is why, after surgery Tommy would not take anything stronger than Advil, even though he was in immense pain! Being a guy, he was going to 'tough it out'! Knowing he was having a rough time Tommy's wife called his sponsor who came by for a chat. He reminded Tommy that "We are not martyrs" and there was nothing wrong with taking the medicine, as long as he followed the doctor's instructions. He suggested that Tommy let his wife hold the pills, and once he started feeling better, to get rid of them!

This was good advice, as the medicine gave Tommy relief from his pain, which helped him to recover from his surgery. Within a few days, the pain lessened and the pills were flushed (this was before we knew how damaging that was).

I remembered Tommy's story many years later, when I had similar surgery. I was very clear with my doctor, letting him know that I was in Recovery and used to take these pills for fun! He only gave me a few, telling me to call if I really needed more. I took about four of them, got rid of the rest, and went on my way.

Then came the warm September afternoon, when I took my four-year-old daughter roller skating at the local rink. We were there with friends, and was something we did often on the weekends. As we made our way around the slower part of the rink (she was four, and I was not very good) she saw one of her friends, and wanted to leave the rink. As we were making our way off, I got hit by a 12-year-old girl and heard a snap!

I spent three days in the hospital, had surgery and was on pain meds, it would have been agony without them. However, I remembered Tommy's story and told the doctor about my Recovery, and once again only got a small number of pills. Thankfully, after a few days at home, I was able to toss these out, and just go on Advil.

Then, a few years ago, I walked out to my car on an icy morning, and wound up in the ER once again! This time with a shattered elbow and an impacted shoulder, which lead to more surgery, and more pain meds! Again, I followed my program and told my doctor the truth, and took the pills as I was instructed...but I was tempted!

This time I was on the Vicodin for about two weeks, both before and after surgery, and it made me a bit nervous. I had to keep them in a secure place, as my daughter was only just out of rehab herself, and I forced myself to get rid of them as soon as I could...but part of me wanted to keep it

I have to admit, that there have been times when I got hurt and wound up in bad pain, I knew that life was going to include a cast, a sling, crutches, and maybe even surgery...yet I could not stop myself from the thought, "I'm gonna get some good drugs"!

But then, this should be expected, as no matter how long we have been Sober we are still Addicts/Alcoholics and hard-wired to use our drug of choice...or any drug for that matter. This is why it is so important to practice our program on a daily basis.

I have also struggled with Anxiety and Depression at times throughout my life, including during my Sobriety – as life does not suddenly become perfect once we become Sober. *Even the Yellow Brick Road was plagued with flying monkeys.* To deal with these issues, I have done counseling and taken medication, always being clear with my doctors about my past abuse of drugs and alcohol. I wanted to ensure that I never took anything that I once used recreationally.

All in all, I equate taking anti-depressants with taking medication for blood pressure, or my asthma.

While it is true that we are not martyrs, we do need to be careful, and keep in mind that we are suffering from an illness that will never go away...another old saying rings true here: "You might get better, but you'll never get well".

Medication can be a good thing, and no one in Recovery should be reluctant to follow a doctor's orders; however, we need to be informed of the risks that some of these drugs pose, and not be afraid to let the doctor know our entire medical history, even the stuff we may not want to admit to.

It is also important to let those around us, those we trust, know what kind of meds we are on, and if the drugs post an exceptional risk (like pain-killers) letting another person to hold on to them for us, to remove some of the temptation to abuse.

Life is good Sober, it is not meant to be a long, slow trudge...though sometimes it certainly can be. We do not want to make things more difficult by playing the martyr, and enduring unnecessary pain; at the same time, we also want to remain vigilant, as the disease of Addiction never takes a day off.

The good news is that Recovery does not take time off either, there is always someone willing and able to help us face the challenges of life, all we need to do is ask for it, and accept it when it is offered.

Together, we can learn how to face any challenge, injury or pain life puts in our way while embracing the true joy of living Sober.

This is a lesson I learned from people in Recovery, like Tommy No Socks and Sunshine Tommy...who embraced the Sober life and wanted everyone else to know the joy for themselves.

9

The Fourteenth Step

I got Sober while living on Staten Island, and working in Manhattan. I went from hitting the bars at lunchtime to going to 12-step meetings that were near work – and this being Manhattan, there were plenty to choose from.

I often went to 74 Below at Trinity Church (which was in a sub-basement), or The Tower Group (which was about half way up one of the World Trade Center towers). However, after about a year of Sobriety I changed jobs and wound up working in Mid-town, in a building at 55th and 6th. There were two meeting nearby, Fog Lifters at 55th and Park, and another at a church on 53rd and Park, so I had all my bases covered! As it was Mid-town, these meetings were usually packed, and we had some interesting speakers, including some that were somewhat well known…leading them to have some pretty good stories.

One of these was a man who was about 80 and had been Sober for 20 years. While he was the grandson of a famous historical figure, this man had a long and storied career of his own. I heard him speaking at a noon meeting in 1992, and during his "qualification" *as we called it back then*, he shared this story, which has stuck with me ever since.

I think of the story whenever I start believe that I have a "lock" on my sobriety, that I have somehow been cured and that I can 'handle it' (sobriety or drinking) on my own.

This is the story as I remember it: there was a new mother, and while she had been concerned that she was drinking too much, the fact that she was able to stop so easily while pregnant led her to believe that she could 'handle it', that it was not such a problem. Besides, now that she was a mother she wouldn't have time to drink, or go out...or have much fun.

And herein lies the problem. After the 'newness' of the baby wore off, the young mother found herself stuck at home, with the baby, for most of her days. It was winter, and the weather was bad and she got a case of cabin fever. Of course, she figured that the best cure was to have a few glasses of wine...after all she could handle it now.

Before long, her drinking was once more getting out of hand, and when she found that it was affecting her ability to care for her baby, and causing trouble in her marriage, she decided to try quitting again. After several unsuccessful attempts, it was suggested that she try going to some 12 Step meetings. She reluctantly agreed to attend a few meetings, but was uncertain as to whether she really needed to be there, she was able to quit many times on her own, why should this time be any different?

After going to the meetings for a few weeks, the young mother felt better, and had managed to stop drinking again; however, she was still not sure she belonged there. When she shared her doubts with a few other sober people, they understood and explained that it was common for new-comers to feel uncertain, to wonder if they really belonged. One friend also pointed out that no one came to these meetings by accident, and that if she was there at the meeting, she was where she was supposed to be.

This sort of made sense to the woman, but she was still uncertain. She continued to debate herself over whether or not she really had a problem, if she really belonged, if she could handle it on her on.

Then, one sunny day in early spring, the young mother skipped her usual Noon Twelve Step meeting and took her baby for a walk up 5th Avenue, along Central Park. It was one of the first warm days of the year and it seemed like everyone was out enjoying the weather. She looked down at her baby sleeping in the stroller and then looked up at the sunlight shining through the new leaves on the trees and felt peaceful for the first time in months.

Suddenly, her serenity was interrupted when an older man lurched out from the shadows of the park! He reeked of whiskey and body odor, having been living in the park for some time. He called to the woman and asked her a question: "What step are you on?" Startled, she asked him "What do you mean?" He smiled at the young mother, and said "I've seen you at those meetings...and I was wondering what step you were on." Realizing that he meant the Twelve Step meetings, she answered him, "Well, I'm pretty new at this, so I guess I am just working on the first three steps, you know, where we admit powerlessness, let go and let God, and turn ourselves over to a higher power." The man nodded, and said, "Good!" Then he asked her another question: "Do you know what step I'm on?" The young mother looked at him, filthy, drunk, and staggering…and she decided to accept his challenge and asked: "Okay, what step are you on?"

The man stopped staggering for a moment, straightened himself up, and a serious look came over his face, "You've heard of the Thirteenth Step, right?" She nodded, "Yes, where someone takes advantage of a new-comer." She had been warned of this step, and the fact that this homeless man brought it up made her nervous. "Well…" he went on, "I'm on the Fourteenth Step: 'Came to believe I could handle it!'" he said with a sigh, and then repeated himself, "Came to believe I could handle it." Then he staggered back into the park and faded into the shadows.

The young mother watched the man walk into the park, and then turned to look at her baby, still sleeping peacefully, and she knew what she had to do.

She turned and walked back down 5th Avenue, turned east onto 55th Street, and arrived at her meeting only 15 minutes late. As she sat down in her seat, with her stroller next to her, the young mother finally felt like she was where she belonged.

And the truth is that no one comes into Recovery by accident, if you think there is a problem…then there is a problem, but there is also help, often closer that you ever expected.

This help can keep all those in Recovery (no matter how many days they have) safe from falling prey to the 14th Step.

About the Author:

 **David Lintvedt** was born in The Bronx, and raised in East Orange, NJ. His adoptive parents were both active in the community and church, and encouraged David to do the same. It is this sense of Community Service, and his experience as person in long-term Recovery, that has led to David's participation Project Live Upper Perk, a grass roots group that seeks to raise awareness, and offer help for, those who are struggling with Substance Use Disorder (Addiction}.

Although the author has had the essay "An Ordinary Adventure" included in the collection: This I Believe: On Fatherhood, and has had other essays which appeared in The Lutheran Magazine and various on-line blogs, this is the first collection of his essays to be published.

David holds a BA in English from Upsala College, and a Master of Divinity from The Lutheran Theological Seminary at Philadelphia. He also has over 30 years of experience in business, and currently works for a major corporation in customer support. He lives in the wilds of Southeastern PA, with his daughter, her boyfriend, a couple of dogs, cats and a gaggle of rabbits...and is regularly inspired and encouraged by his long-time Significant Other.

20880465R00092

Made in the USA
Middletown, DE
11 December 2018